GREEK GRAMMAR

YOU *CAN* LEARN BIBLE GREEK

A Clear Introductory Course

BY

JOHN POLY

POLYKARPOS PUBLISHING
711 E MAIN STREET #333
RIVERTON, WY 82501

GREEK GRAMMAR

YOU CAN LEARN BIBLE GREEK!

A Clear, Introductory Course

BY JOHN POLY

PUBLISHED BY:

POLYKARPOS PUBLISHING
711 E MAIN STREET #333
RIVERTON, WY 82501

Library of Congress Control Number: 2003110560
Poly, John
Greek Grammar, You Can Learn Bible Greek! A Clear, Introductory Course
by John Poly
ISBN 0-9744525-0-5

Cover design by Veronica Martinez

TABLE OF CONTENTS

TABLE OF CONTENTS
(CONTINUED)

Chapter: Page Number:

The author of this publication is pleased to make it available. Its purpose is to make Bible **(*Koine*)** Greek understandable for those who wish to learn this wonderful language. At the same time, those with some knowledge of Greek can increase their comprehension of grammar, and thus improve their skills.

Possessing a basic knowledge of Greek, can be a valuable asset. To open a Greek interlinear* of the ***"New Testament"*** and to read it with clear understanding, is a lifetime dream which most of us have entertained. Can *you* acquire such an ability? Yes! This author believes you *can* learn Bible Greek!

Do not feel that a formal education in Greek is required in order achieve such a noble feat. No doubt choosing and devoting oneself to an education by trained scholars possessing degrees in Greek may offer you a distinct advantage. Yet, because of the personal circumstances of the average person, many find this pursuit nearly impossible to undertake.

Living at a time when learning at home is becoming increasingly popular and practical, education in Greek in the privacy of one's own study or den has been pursued with great success. With the proper tools, including personal discipline, home instruction will enable the student to read and understand the *basics* of his or her Greek interlinear in a surprisingly short period of time. This, of course, does not mean one's grasp of Greek will come instantaneously, but along with an step-by-step guide, you will notice fine progress even after a few exercises.

(*A Greek-English interlinear is a word-for-word translation of the "New Testament", containing English words under each Greek word and phrase.)

There is a great challenge for an author to present information on on a subject of this nature. Nevertheless, Greek grammar does not have to be beyond the mental grasp of any of us. If it is presented in such a way that captures and maintains the reader's interest, the author has accomplished his purpose. It is the opinion of this author that Greek can be made understandable, and it might be added, most enjoyable and engrossing. Yes, if you are eager to do so, you ***can*** learn ***Koine,*** or, Bible Greek!

You may wonder if modern Greek is different from ***Koine*** Greek. They are not exactly the same. Yet, amazingly, there is a great similarity between the two. It is surprising to see words which have been preserved in the ***"New Testament,"*** and which are in common use in Greek of the modern day. A few examples are: *"apostolos"* (apostles), *"biblio"* (book), *"theos"* (God), *"kyrios"* (Lord), *"ecclesia"* (church, or congregation), and *"kosmos"* (world), *"diabolos"* (devil), *"ge"* (earth), *"ouranos"* (heaven), *"pneuma"* (spirit), *"psykhe"* (soul), and *"adelphos"* (brother).

One study of the 28 chapters of the book of Matthew alone shows that almost 820 principal words are retained in modern Greek Bibles. The Lord's Prayer is strikingly similar. This is significant, because ***"New Testament"*** Greek in its entirety, contains only 5600 words, including proper names.(For some examples, see Matt. 7:15; 9:37; 13:21,30, 37-39; Mark 4:28; 7:3,4; Luke 1:2,10)

Studies into the history of the Greek language reveal that modern Greek makes a *direct connection* with the ***Koine*** Greek. For example, it has been observed that the Greek spoken today in some villages of Greece has had far less change in the last 2,200 years than the Greek which was spoken in the previous 650 years.

Some may find this fact difficult to accept. However, one noted scholar remarked there is a noticeable likeness between the spoken ***Koine*** of the first century and the everyday speech of modern Greek. This is startling, since English has made stark changes in speech and writing within the last *700 years!*

You may be very excited about your pursuit of Greek and may wish to invest in numerous lexicons and grammar books. But that can be an expensive investment. For starters, you will find it practical to purchase two or three books dealing with *basic* Greek grammar. Later, as you progress in your understanding of Greek, you may wish to purchase advanced publications, or get them through your local library on a limited loan basis.

Some important points the author wishes to stress: Studying Greek grammar would not be properly undertaken if one tries to use it as a means of gaining a marked advantage over others, with the intent of winning a theological argument. Greek lexicographers note that grammar is not always the final word for theology. Often, it is the context which determines the meaning. Your reason for learning Greek should be to enhance your increased understanding of the Bible and should be employed as a fine supplement to Bible reading. Greek must not be used in an attempt to squeeze out of the Bible a personal interpretation. In turn, you can use what you have acquired to help others. It requires diligence to learn Greek so that you can understand what *it* says, not what *you* want it to say. Be honest with your discoveries, and accept them. Hence, to learn the accurate meaning of Greek, you have to give it the time and effort it deserves. It's a beautiful language- very expressive in revealing the spiritual treasures of God's Word.

It will not be overnight that you will acquire a working knowledge of Greek. However, what the author has acquired are methods which make learning more enjoyable. Being able to stand between the English and Greek, you will be able to demonstrate to yourself in very simple terms, how to explain the meaning of both languages. You will see how even your knowledge of the principles of English, or your own native tongue, becomes easier to explain when you undertake a study of Greek.

So, do not be discouraged if you have tried to learn Greek by means of other primers and grammars, only to end up frustrated, and thinking: "I *can't* learn Greek." Yes, you can, if the teaching is made uncomplicated and enjoyable. If you are willing- and patient, the author is ready to teach you in a progressive manner, so that you will confidently say, even after a few lessons, "I *can* learn! I *am* learning Greek!"

Moving progressively into a new century and millennium, and having already faced a variety of challenges and tragedies, we can be confident that knowledge regarding vital subjects will continue to increase, and that we will be able to achieve our desired goals. May you embark upon this lofty pursuit of understanding ***Koine*** Greek, and find great pleasure in knowing more accurately the true sayings of God.

September, 2003 John Poly

ACKNOWLEDGMENTS

*The author wishes to express his deepest appreciation for the brilliant work of many Bible scholars, who, through the years, have published grammars, lexicons, interlinears, and other works, for serious students of **Koine** Greek.*

The author is also greatly indebted to the wonderfully artistic services of Deborah Walter, who has lovingly provided most of the beautiful illustrations for this grammar, which enhance its desirability as an effective teaching manual.

Special thanks also to Paula Ness, who has supplied the supplementary art within the following pages, including the anatomy figure at the end of this publication, identifying body components in Greek.

Deepest gratitude goes to my family, especially my devoted wife Dona, who encouraged me through this monumental project from start to finish.

*Above all, "thanks to God through Jesus Christ our Lord!" (Romans 7:25) for including, among His many gifts, His inspired Word containing the wonderfully expressive language of **Koine** Greek.*

NOTICE OF DISCLAIMER

This publication is provided for the sole purpose of acquainting intereste readers with Bible Greek. The publisher and author does not intend that it be considered as a substitute for theological training in a seminar or university. Neither should it be expected that the author will grant professional services regarding the subjects covered in this primer.

It is also the objective of this publication to REFRAIN from considering controversial subjects on Bible passages. It has purposely kept clear of such material, so that the student can concentrate on the vital principles of Greek grammar. Therefore, the author will refuse to acknowledge all correspondence concerning religious doctrines and debates over words.

References in this grammar to other scholars' research on specific point concerning *Koine* ***Greek grammar can be verified by one's own study in other sources, whether through the library, bookstores, or on the Interne***

The author and publisher has endeavored to make this introductory course as complete and accurate as possible, having made a close study o numerous grammars, lexicons, and Greek interlinears, for the purpose o making basic *Koine* ***Greek pleasurable and instructive. Artwork include is strictly a teaching tool, and is not intended to promote any particular ideology. Humor in the illustrations is meant to add interest to the study.***

This textbook on Greek grammar, while agreeing in substance, does not directly quote from any published Greek interlinears, grammars or lexicons, but translates the Greek of the "New Testament" into English a accurately as possible, according to the author's study of *Koine* ***Greek.***

The purpose of this book has been to assist you to learn the fundamental of *Koine* ***Greek. Neither the author nor Polykarpos Publishing shall be held liable or responsible regarding any loss or damage incurred, directly or indirectly, by the material contained within this publication.***
If you do not wish to agree to the above, you may return this primer to the publisher for a full refund.

CHAPTER ONE

INTRODUCTION TO BIBLE GREEK

Diving for pearls in deep, clear seas. We can use this expression to describe your quest to discover precious truths embedded within the Greek text of the Holy Scriptures.

Since ancient times, courageous and determined divers would plunge into the tropical waters of the world's seas, hoping to find these beautiful gems locked within the shells of oysters. Bright pearls of glorious shades have come to light and are highly treasured.

However, for many centuries, the possession of pearls was generally limited to royalty and the well-to-do.

It was the same with ***Koine*** Greek. Having been the international tongue in the days of Christ and his apostles, it was gradually replaced by Latin, and other languages. However, Greek endures as a living tongue to this day.

In the centuries that followed the original writings of the *"New Testament,"* manuscript copies continued to be written in Greek, then Latin. Yet, when Latin died out, influential rulers opposed any translation of the Bible into the languages of the common man. But this time, humble people were not to be deprived of precious "pearls," namely, Scriptural truths.

Gradually, by the 16th century these valuable "gems" became available to all hungering for the Bible. Translation of Scripture into the vernacular made it possible for anyone to gain an accurate knowledge of the Word of God.

Today, the average person can greatly increase his understanding of the Sacred Scriptures, and so, obtain a more accurate meaning of the Greek text.

Our desire to know more is peaked when see ourselves moving well into a new century and millennium, perhaps anticipating the fulfillment of significant Bible prophecies.

So, then, we invite you to come into the exciting world of **Koine** Greek, and be prepared to dive into the crystal clear waters of God's Word to discover its beautiful "pearls."

In this grammar, we provide a step-by-step method by which you will *quickly* grasp the principles of Greek. They are like pieces in a puzzle, carefully explained in simple terms.

You will be taught by ***three*** outstanding teaching aids, which will make learning interesting:

1- ILLUSTRATIONS: Pictures, drawings and graphs are added to the text, and will assist you to put the pieces of the puzzle together. They will help you reason on the points considered so you can recall the various aspects of grammar.

Some may find these illustrations too simplistic, even childish. But we must remember, when we first learned our language, understanding came easy when we followed this method. It was also instructive, which built up our self-confidence.

2- ASSOCIATION: This second teaching aid is also valuable. Associating Greek with things with which we are familiar will further our knowledge, making Greek more easily understood. Have you ever looked up a word in the dictionary, and often found it has a Greek root?

As examples: the Greek word "psyche", meaning "soul," is used in the English word "psychiatry." The study of anthropology comes from two Greek words: "anthropos" (man), and "logos" (study).

Association with familiar words in Greek will be a great aid in our studies.

3- EXERCISE: You will learn very quickly as you begin to use the principles taught in this grammar. You will observe periodic exercises through your primer *which you must use* if you are to benefit fully from the instructions contained herein. This is where you must do your part. It will not take you as long as you may think to use this third aid. Learning Greek is lots of fun, but you can't rush it.

It is understandable how anxious you are to learn, but there are no shortcuts. You cannot expect miracles and feel the book will do all the thinking for you. This grammar is an instruction guide, and a memory aid, but you have to do the work.

You must become familiar with the Greek characters and their sounds if you are to be successful in learning Bible Greek. Take the time to learn. It may try your patience, but it's worth your time and effort.

Use your imagination. For instance, the Greek letter *gamma* (γ) may seem to have no familiarity to English. Well, look closely at the letter and see what it may resemble. Do you see a sea gull in flight? When you see *gamma*, you can think of the letter "g" for gull, and that tells you it is pronounced as the letter "g". O.K., that may not be what you see, but whatever you see, associate that mental picture with the letter.

Or, take the letter *theta* (θ). Perhaps you can view it as a throne. You can say the throne has an oval back, as shown by the shape of the letter *theta,* and the horizontal bar within the letter is the king's seat. Hence, *theta* (θ) can be identified by the word "throne."

(Other examples: *delta* (δ) can be a duck, for the letter "d"; *zeta* (ζ) can be a zig-zag, for the letter "z"; *eta* (η), an egret feeding in water for the long "e" sound; *lambda* (λ) can be a ladder for the letter "l"; *my* (μ), mountain peaks for "m"; and *pi* (π), a plateau for the letter "p.")

Use whatever helps you to remember, but as you can see, letting your imagination go to work, adds pleasure to it.

To make your studies pleasing to the eye, we set our format in large print. This makes the lessons easy to read, and helpful in examining carefully the presently unfamiliar Greek characters of the alphabet. As a result, you will find yourself absorbed in your study.

Well, here we are: At the edge of the crystal clear waters of Bible Greek. Do you have your equipment ready? Are you determined to find something? Then, dive in and discover your precious "pearls" of truth.

CHAPTER 2

THE GREEK ALPHABET

(With Pronunciation Key)

Capital Letters	Small Letters	Name	Pronunciation
Α	α	*al'pha*	***a*** *as in "father"*
Β	β	*be'ta*	***b*** *or soft "v"*
Γ	γ	*gam'ma*	*gutteral "**g**"*
Δ	δ	*del'ta*	*"**d**" or soft "**th**"*
Ε	ε	*e' psi lon*	*short "**e**" (met)*
Ζ	ζ	*ze' ta*	*z*
Η	η	*e' ta*	*long "**e**" ("we")*
Θ	θ	*the' ta*	***th*** *as in "theatre"*
Ι	ι	*i o' ta*	***i*** *as in "machine"*
Κ	κ	*kap'pa*	***k***
Λ	λ	*lam' bda*	***l*** *as in "lion"*
Μ	μ	*my*	***m***
Ν	ν	*ny*	***n***
Ξ	ξ	*xi*	***ks*** *as in "accent"*
Ο	ο	*o' mi kron*	***o*** *as in "Lord"*
Π	π	*pi*	***p*** *or soft "b"*
Ρ	ρ	*hro*	***r*** *(rolled)*

(Alphabet Continues on the Next Page)

CAPITAL	SMALL	NAME	PRONUNCIATIO
Σ	σ, ς *(final)*	*sig' ma*	***s***
Τ	τ	*tau*	***t***
Υ	υ	*y' psi lon*	***y** sound in on*
Φ	φ	*phi*	***ph** as in phon*
Χ	χ	*khi*	*gutteral **k***
Ψ	ψ	*psi*	***ps** as in lips*
Ω	ω	*o me' ga*	***o** as in note*

(This grammar utilizes modern Greek pronunciations. Greek scholars comment that ***Koine*** Greek is not exactly the same as modern Greek, but tends to veer towards it.)

A. DIPHTHONGS

A diphthong is *two vowels together in one syllable* to produce one sound.

For example, in English, the two vowels "e" and "a" together produce the long "e" sound in "teach;" It is similar in Greek. Below, we list the more common Greek diphthongs and their sounds. Familiarize yourself with each of them:

Greek Diphthong	*Pronunciation*
αι	*Short "**e**" as in "w**e**t"*
αυ	*"**af**" as in "**aw**ful"*
*ει**	*long "**e**" as in "**ei**ther"*
ευ	*"**ev**" as in "**ev**er"*
*οι**	*long "**e**" as in "h**e**"*
ου	*long "**u**" as in "**you**"*
*υι**	*"**y**" sound as in "**y**oke" or long "e"*

(*Note the similar pronunciation between these diphthongs and the letters *"e' ta"*, *"i·o' ta"*, and *"y' psi·lon")*

The pronunciations of Greek letters and diphthongs in this primer are according to modern Greek. Other grammars may use different pronunciations, but what we have chosen is in agreement with the pronunciations of the period leading up and through to the First Century of the Common Era. Scholars observe the use of the long "e" sound in these letters and diphthongs even before the Greek Scriptures of the Christian era were written. They call the process **"itacism." (pronounced **"ee'** ta- sizm," the pronunciation of the Greek letter **"e' ta"** in modern Greek to sound as the English long "e").*

B. ACCENTS

There are *three* kinds of accent in Greek:

(a) The *acute* (´) as in λόγος ***("word")***

(b) The *grave* (`) as in αὐτὸς* ἔλεγεν ***("he said.")***

(*In many instances, a word with an *acute* accent on the last syllable, changes to one with a *grave* accent when it is before other words in the same sentence.)

(c) The *circumflex* (῀) as in δοῦλος ***("slave")***

The accent sign stands over the vowel of the accented syllable as shown here:

ἀ γά πη (a ***ga'*** pe) - "love"

"Learn the accents and know where they are placed."

(**Note**: In Greek, the vowel remains *short* and is not long when accented. The rule of making long the accented vowel applies only to proper nouns which are translated from other languages ***into English.*** The long and short sounds of the words in Greek are governed by the sounds of the *letters* and *diphthongs* themselves. The accent indicates which syllable should be stressed.)

Concerning Greek *accents*, the last syllable of a word is called the *ultima;* the next-to-the-last syllable is referred to as the *penult;* and the one before the penult is named the *antepenult*.

An Example: ἀλήθεια *("truth")*

ἀ	λή	θει*	α
	antepenult	*penult*	*ultima*

A rule to remember regarding accents: No accent can stand farther back than the third syllable from the end of the word, as noted in the above example.

The Greek acute accent mark **(′)** is similar to the accent mark in English. But the grave accent mark is shown the opposite way **(`)**. The circumflex **(⁀),** is quite different than the others.

They identify certain words which can only be distinguished by their accents, as well as their positions in a sentence. More on this in later studies.

*(*ει forms a diphthong, giving a long "e" sound. When the Greek vowels, such as iota (ι) do not form a diphthong with the preceding vowel, two dots, which are called **diaeresis,** are written over it; as in ἀλληλούϊα ("a-lee-loo'-**ya**"). The iota with two dots above it becomes a "y," and is pronounced **"ya."** (See Revelation 19:1)*

C. ASPIRATION

There are two *breathings* in Greek, the *rough* breathing, which is identified by this mark (῾) over the beginning vowel, as in ᾅδης* ("**H**ades," Rev. 20:14); and the *smooth* breathing, identified by the mark (᾿) over the beginning vowel, as in the word ἄνθρωπος* ("man," John 19:5); In the first example, "**H**ades" is *aspirated,* which means it is given a rough breathing by placing the letter ***"h"*** before the vowel; In the second, "anthropos" is smooth and remains *unaspirated* (without the "h").

(*In these cases, both the aspiration and accent marks appear over the same letter.)

(Other examples: ὥρα ("**h**ora,") *hour*, at Matt. 14:15, and ἔχω ("ekho") *I have*, at John 5:36).

Aspiration marks also appear over the *second* vowel of words as in αὐτός ("he"), because these form **diphthongs.**

*"Look for the words **aspiring** for recognition."*

Aspiration is an interesting point of Greek grammar, and you will find it quite useful in your study of *Koine* Greek.

CHAPTER 3

IDENTIFYING GREEK WORDS

Now that we are getting more familiar with the sounds of the Greek *letters, diphthongs,* their *accents*, and *aspirations,* let us put our knowledge to work.

As you begin this study, you will discover the exciting use of the ***Koine*** (which is pronounced "Kee-***nee'*** "), or Common Greek, and which was expressed on occasion by God's Son, during his zealous ministry in the land of Palestine, where Aramaic, Hebrew and Greek were spoken.

You will also begin to understand the words of the apostle Paul and other disciples of Christ, who translated into Greek, words Jesus expressed, and which are now a part of the Sacred Scriptures.

Olive trees adorn the beautiful landscape of Palestine.

It was on the Mount of Olives where Jesus gave his apostles the distinctive sign of his future "parousia," or, presence.

A) *A SIMPLE EXERCISE:*

Let us begin with a common noun in Greek, ***the·os'***, the Greek word for **God,** as found at John 3:16. (Note the pronunciation and the accent. How would you pronounce it?)

1. *GOD* - θεός ("The·**os'** ")

Here is a breakdown of the word. Pronounce each letter several times. Look back at the pronunciation key if necessary.

θ - theta

ε - epsilon

ο - omicron

ς - sigma

θεός was often used in classical Greek literature to describe gods such as Zeus and Hermes. In the "New Testament," lexicons typically describe θεός as a general classification of divinities and potentates, with primary reference to Almighty God.

(***the os'*** would, therefore be pronounced "theh-***os,*** " - NOT "**thee'** os"; Observe the short "e" [epsilon], with the accent on the last syllable.)

2. Here is a noun from John 1:1 identifying the role of God's Son in heaven:

Word - λόγος ("**Lo'** gos")

Once again, we provide you with a breakdown of the word under consideration:

λ - lambda

ο - omicron

γ - gamma

ο - omicron

ς - (ending) sigma

Codices, early manuscript volumes of the "New Testament" in book form, are available to compare with our modern Bibles. Scholars of the Greek text generally agree that the text is virtually sound, and has been excellently transmitted through the centuries of time to our day.

In this word, the accent is on the ***first*** syllable; the two vowel sounds of both syllables use the Greek letter "omicron" (meaning "*the little one.*"). They both have the sound of "o" as in the English word "Lord". λό γος (**Lo'** gos)

IDENTIFYING MORE GREEK WORDS

Here are more Greek words from John 1:1. If you have a Greek Interlinear of the *New Testament*, you can see them in the Greek text yourself. (Check with your local bookstore if you need to acquire a Greek interlinear. It will prove to be a valuable investment)

Read the following word and say it out loud:

3. *and* - καί ("keh")

κ - kappa

α - alpha

ι - iota

"Familiarize yourself with these words. They will build your self-confidence."

The letter "kappa" is like the English letter "k." The diphthong in καί is αι (alpha and iota combined). Now look back at the pronunciation key The diphthong αι sounds like a short "e"; thus, we would say **"keh"**.

Let's study one more Greek word from John 1:1:

4. to, toward - πρός ("pros")

π - pi

ρ - rho

ο - omicron

ς - sigma

πρός (pros) is a preposition and it indicates the relationship of words in the sentence.

Hence, we would say in Greek: "John was *to,* or, *toward* his father," or, when translated, "John was *with* his father." It means being turned *in the direction of someone* or, *toward* that one.

Of course, the **case** in which the preposition πρός finds itself, determines the translation. (More on **cases** in the next chapter, and on **prepositions** in Chapter 7.)

Now that you are mastering the use of Greek letters, you can concentrate on another Greek phenomenon:

Greek nouns like "God" (Gr- θεός) can be seen in *another form* to express their relation to other words

(A) Each noun has a fundamental part called the ***stem;***

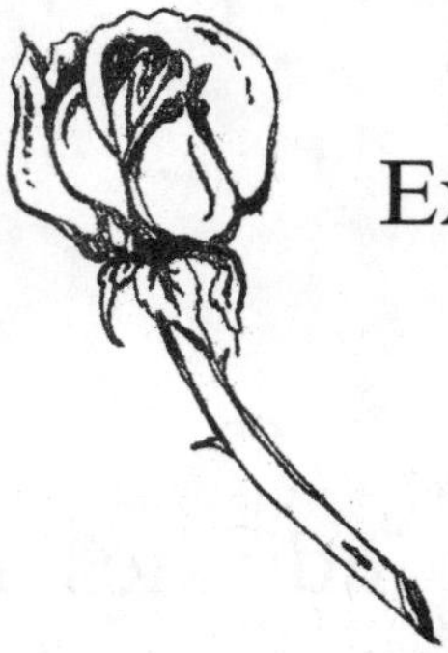

Example: θεός ("the•os' ") has a part that remains the same, as noted below:

θε is the *stem* of θεός

Think about the stem of a flower; its basic part.

Greek has words that have a basic part which always remains the same, as we have in English:

We describe a **man** and a wo**man,** the human race as **man**kind, one's traits as **man**ly, etc.

Our next chapter will observe these *variations* in Greek as we discuss **Nouns.**

CHAPTER 4
Nouns In Greek

Θεός is a common noun in the Greek text. We will demonstrate using *forms* of this word for illustration.

Turn to John 1:1 to see a *different form* of θεός :

πρὸς τὸν θεόν
(to) toward the God
(Notice, not θεός, but θεόν)

Note, too, how the article (τὸν) ends the same as the noun θεόν. This shows they are **related** to one another in the sentence. The preposition πρός is responsible for making this difference*.

Thus, πρὸς τὸν θεόν (*"to, toward the God"*) is a **related phrase** and shows the words **belong** to one another in that phrase.

Scholars call these inflections or changes* *"declensions."*** *Nouns, the article, adjectives and pronouns are declined. In this grammar, the author will at times use the declensions appearing in Greek interlinears, while at other times, employing the undeclined forms of these words appearing in lexicons.*

(C) But the original *form* for "God," (Greek- θεός) reveals that the noun, in this instance, is **not** declined or inflected.

*"For **Names,** I'm your Man!"*

θεός is in the ***Nominative Case***.
(*pronounced "Nom'-na-tive"*)
It is the *"Naming Case."*

It means the noun is the case of the *subject*, and remains unaltered in contrast with the other cases

This **case** differs from other **cases** in that it is not governed by other words; or, put another way: a noun is not placed in the nominative case due to the influence of any other word(s) upon it.

Nouns, also called *substantives,* simply name a person, place, thing, or quality.

The Greek nouns θεός and λόγος remain in their undeclined forms in the ***nominative case.*** Nouns in other ***cases*** are changed, due to being influenced by words, such as prepositions.

2. FIVE CASES IN GREEK

A. When the noun θεόν (form of θεός) is governed by other words, it is not nominative, but is in ***another case.***

1. θεός is in the ***Nominative Case.***

2. θεόν is in the ***Accusative Case***.

Grammarians have named this second case *Accusative,* because, as in this example, it points the article or preposition *"to" or "toward"* the noun (as in θεόν, a form of θεός).

Example: πρὸς > τὸν > θεόν·
(to) toward > the > God.

*"Let me **extend** the idea In **this** direction."*

The *Accusative case,* however, has nothing to do with accusation. Scholars call it the case of *extension*, because it measures direction (as noted above), or content (*how much*), or scope (*how far*, or *how long a time*).

B. *Three other cases* of the noun explain its relationship to other words in the sentence.

They are as follows:

3. ***Genitive Case***
(Case of Kind, or Source)

Example: ἡ εἰρήνη τοῦ θεοῦ
(Phil. 4:7) the peace the of God
1 2 4 3 5

(The Numbers indicate the order in which the words read in English)

Note: τοῦ θεοῦ
the of God
2 1 3

Nouns in the ***genitive case*** mostly end in οῦ (Pronounced "oo" as in "you")

These Greek letters are omicron (ο) and y'psilon (υ).

Nouns in the ***genitive case*** are usually associated with the prepositions **"from"** and **"of "**; They *specify* or identify *kind* or *source.*

(a) They can refer to *possession:*

τὸν οἶκον τοῦ πατρός μου

the house **of** my Father JOHN 2:16

(That is, what the Father *possesses* or *owns.*)

(b) Or, they can be discussing *origin (subjective):*

δικαιοσύνη γὰρ θεοῦ

the righteousness for **of God** ROM. 1:17

(That is, the righteousness which comes *from* God.)

(c) They can also refer to *object (objective):*

ἡ φιλία τοῦ κόσμου

the friendship **of the** world. JAMES 4:4

(That is, the world is the *object* of one's affections.)

(Note: The Greek diphthong ου *is a clue to identifying nouns in the masculine and neuter genders in the* ***genitive case****.)*

There are other forms of the ***genitive case***, but what is provided here should be a good starting point.

4. *Dative Case*
(Case of Personal Interest)

*"Please be assured that I **do** take a personal interest in you."*

Example: τῷ Θεῷ
to the God. **John 16:2**

Nouns in the ***dative case*** often end with the Greek letter *omega* **(ω)** (long "o").

Words in the ***dative case*** use the prepositions **"to"**, and **"for"**, but more as indicators of *attention, benefit, or possession* of a subject.

Greek lexicons describe this case as one which shows personal interest, and which lays stress on a *person's* advantage or disadvantage.

We may say in English "Thanks ***to*** you", which stresses advantage, and interest in *you*; That is how the ***dative case*** is used;

Example: πιστὴν τῷ κυρίῳ
(Acts 16:15) faithful **to** the Lord

It shows *personal attention* in the subject.

5. *VOCATIVE CASE*

(Case of Address)

Example: πάτερ, κύριε τοῦ οὐρανοῦ
Father, lord of the heaven

καὶ τῆς γῆς,
and the earth, **(Matthew 11:25)**

Nouns in the ***Vocative*** Case use the ***Nominative*** Case as noted above;

The ***Vocative*** is not actually a case, but Greek scholars differentiate it because it is used in *forms of address.*

Another Example:

"In ***case*** *you wonder, I'm very* ***vocal.****"*

Θεέ μου, θεέ μου, ἵνα
God of me, God of me, for purpose
τί με ἐγκατέλιπες;
what me did you forsake? **(MATTHEW 27:46)**

(Note how θεός changes to θεέ here. (short "e")

"THEOU"* REVIEW

Let us see what we have learned so far:

1- Which letters and dipthongs contain the long "e" sound? (Answer on Pages 17-19)

2- What is the symbol of the Greek letter sigma, but what is its ending symbol? (Answer- Page 18)

3- How is the diphthong "ai" pronounced? (Answer- Pages 19& 26)

4- Give the three kinds of accents and where they are located in Greek words. (Answer- Pages 20 & 21)

5- What are aspiration and unaspiration, and by what marks are they identified? (Answer- Page 22)

6- What does the word *Koine* mean? (Answer- Page 23)

7- Name the five Greek cases and how they decline the noun θεός (the·os'). Answer- Pages 29-35)

Well, how did we do? Fine, we're sure.

(*"*Theou*" - "God" in the genitive case.)

CHAPTER 5

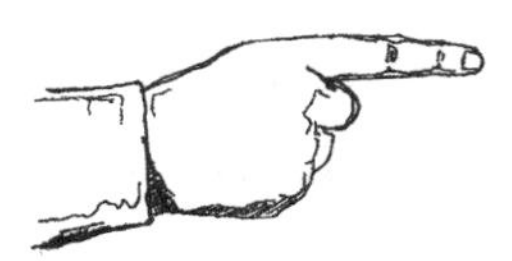

THE ARTICLE

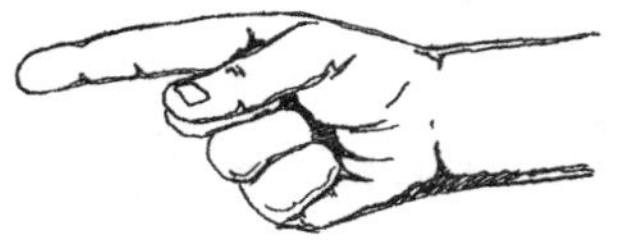

In Greek, as in English, the article **"the"** (Greek- ὁ, pronounced "ho") appears before a number of words and makes these words definite.

For Example: **(John 1:14)**

Καὶ	ὁ	λόγος	σὰρξ	ἐγένετο
And	**the**	Word	flesh	became

(**Note:** The article "the" before "Word" points as an index finger toward *someone in particular.*)

Another Example: **(Mark 3:31)**

ἡ	μήτηρ	αὐτοῦ	καὶ	οἱ	ἀδελφοὶ	αὐτοῦ
the	mother	of him	and	**the**	brothers	of him

(**Note:** The article "the" before "mother" (ἡ) is in the *feminine* gender, while the article "the" before "brothers" (οἱ) is in the *masculine* gender, but is in the *plural* number.)

In each case, *certain individuals* are identified, and the article in these instances is used as a *pointer* to make clear the subject(s) discussed.

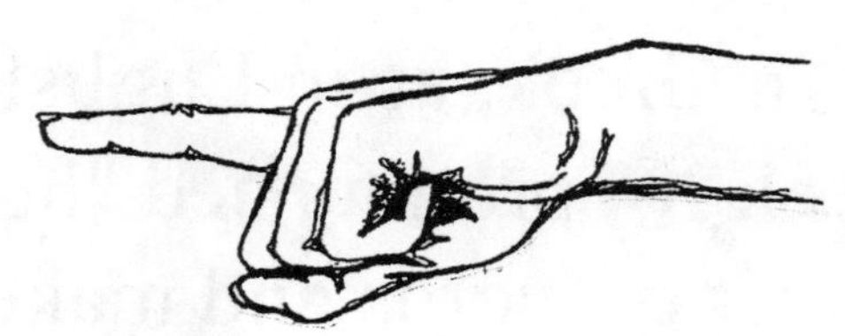

A. DECLENSION OF THE DEFINITE ARTICLE

The definite article is declined or *changed*, the same as a noun is changed, to agree with number, gender and case.

For instance, while we may say ὁ θεός (*ho theos,'* "the God," nominative case), we can say τὸν θεόν *(ton theon'*, "the God," accusative case).

Both the article and noun agree in **case** as they do in **person** and **number**

It is beneficial for you to become familiar with the *variations* in which the Greek article is expressed in the Greek Scriptures.

Note below the *declensions* of the definite article:

SINGULAR NUMBER

CASE -	Nominative:	Genitive:	Dative:	Accusative:
Masculine Gender -	***ὁ***	***τοῦ***	***τῷ***	***τόν***
Feminine Gender -	***ἡ***	***τῆς***	***τῇ***	***τήν***
Neuter Gender -	***τό***	***τοῦ***	***τῷ***	***τό***
English Translation -	***the***	***of the***	***to the***	***the***

PLURAL NUMBER

Case:	Nominative:	Genitive:	Dative:	Accusative:
Masculine Gender -	***οἱ***	***τῶν***	***τοῖς***	***τούς***
Feminine Gender -	***αἱ***	***τῶν***	***ταῖς***	***τάς***
Neuter Gender -	***τά***	***τῶν***	***τοῖς***	***τά***
English Translation -	***the***	***of the***	***to the***	***the***

Note: The definite article does not include a *vocative* case; Hence, when someone or thing is addressed, the *nominative* case is used instead.

Remember: There are *three genders* in Greek: masculine, feminine and neuter, which agree in number and case with the article and noun.

For examples in your Greek interlinear, note Luke 8:38 ("the man," *singular, masculine*) and Luke 11:31 ("the men," *plural, masculine*) where forms of the article are used in the charts above.

The *neuter* gender of the article is used in instances where *impersonal things* are mentioned:

ἐν τῷ ἀγρῷ
in the field. **MATTHEW 24:40**

(NOTE: Both article and noun above are in the dative case.)

(See also John 11:55, τὸ [and] τοῦ πάσχα, *the Passover.*)

The Greek article also uses *personal gender* when it is applied to impersonal things, as you will see at Mark 11:13; Luke 21:21; John 13:5; Acts 8:14; and Ephesians 1:13.

(More on this subject when we discuss Greek pronouns.)

B. THE ABSENCE OF THE ARTICLE

This is one of the most often undervalued aspects of Greek grammar, but is one of the most vital.

There are a number of reasons for the *absence** of the article in Greek. Here are a few:

(1) The article is absent when a noun is governed by a *preposition*. For example:

John 1:1		Mark 15:21	
Ἐν	ἀρχῇ	ἀπ'	ἀγροῦ
In	beginning	from	field

It is obvious in these instance, the article "the" must be supplied when translating into English.

When the Greek Bible writer used the *preposition,* he did not place the article before the noun. In this case, the reader would understand and supply it.

(* *We use the phrase "**absence** of the article," rather than to say "the aricle was **omitted,**" because the Bible writer often saw no need to include it. Scholars agree with our conclusion.)*

(2) The article is sometimes absent with nouns that are the *only things* of their *kinds*.

Example: **Luke 21:25**

ἐν ἡλίῳ* καὶ σελήνῃ* καὶ ἄστροις
in sun, and moon, and stars.

*(*The small mark under these letters is called an **iota subscript,** and is transliterated from Greek with the letter. So ῳ becomes **oi,** and ῃ is **ei.**)*

(But note Matthew 24:29 where sun, moon and stars each *have* the article. The difference is Luke's account contains a *prepositional phrase* which does *not* utilize the definite article.)

(3) Proper Names are often without the article in Greek.

For a number of examples, check the names given at 2 Timothy 4:9-21, using a Greek Interlinear translation. There you will see the names of Demas, Crescens, Titus, and others mentioned with no article before each name in the Greek text.

Once more, this is not an inflexible rule. Names *with* the article are also found in Greek. (See Matthew 2:1,3; 3:6; Acts 7:30; 1 Cor. 10:18)

(4) When the Noun is *indefinite*, or *describes* the subject, as in a simple predicate phrase.

Δαιμόνιον ἔχεις· **John 7:20**
a demon you are possessing.

(Note: "a" is supplied before "demon" when translating into English.)

Another example: **LUKE 23:6**

Γαλιλαῖός ἐστιν,
a Galilean is,

(Also, Acts 16:3; 19:34; 22:26,27,29; 23:27)

These are what scholars call simple predicate phrases in the nominative case. The verb is a linking verb from the subject to the predicate, and is called a *copula*. (Latin- "to join")

There are myriads of instances in the Greek text where the article is *absent* and where English translators have properly supplied the indefinite articles *"a"* or *"an"* before a word. They have done so in some 200 places in Acts of Apostles alone! (We give this book as typical of what *you* will find as you examine the Greek Scripture text).

Scholars understand there is no *"a"* or *"an"* before nouns in *Koine* Greek, but feel perfectly justified to insert these *indefinite articles* to make the sense clear when translating into English and other languages.

This they will do *if* they believe the subject is *indefinite* or is a *description.* This practice is deemed appropriate and is viewed as an individual judgment.

*As for other examples, see where translators added **"an"** before nouns at: Matthew 9:16; 2 Corinthians 1:1; Galatians 1:8; 2:5; Rev. 13:9.*

There are other reasons for the Greek article's absence, but what we have included here will give you a taste of Greek expression. Later studies will examine all of these in detail.

Without a doubt, students of Greek must exercise caution in determining whether the English indefinite articles "a" or "an" should be used when the article is absent in Greek.

Accuracy in rendering the Greek text into another language is imperative, and it must be consistent with the *context* of the word or phrase under consideration as well as its *history.* The translator's rendering of a passage should also be in *harmony* with the teachings of the entire Bible.

There is no doubt that grammar regarding the Greek article and its absence is important to our study of Bible Greek.

C. POSITION OF THE ARTICLE

We shall take a moment and examine where the article is positioned in a sentence.

We see it before the adjective and the noun, as at James 2:7: τὸ καλὸν ὄνομα, *"the noble name."*

We observe the article twice: once before the adjective, and once before the noun, at John 10:11: ὁ ποιμὴν ὁ καλός, *"the exquisite shepherd."*

We find the article with each of three adjectives in succession, as at Revelation 1:17, 18: ὁ πρῶτος καὶ ὁ ἔσχατος, καὶ ὁ ζῶν, *"the First and the Last and the living one."*

The article is seen with anarthrous nouns (nouns without the article), while the attribute has the article, as at Romans 8:33: θεὸς ὁ δικαιῶν, *"God the (one) pronouncing just."*

The article is unique, and is a vital part of Greek grammar. As you comprehend its use, you will learn to appreciate its value and purpose.

CHAPTER 6
VERBS

As with English, Greek verbs are *action* words. However, Greek verbs do *not* strictly have reference to *time*, or *tense.*

In Greek tenses*, it is the ***kind of action*** that is stressed, while the time element is given minimum consideration.

Koine Greek uses *two* verb-types:

One denoting momentary, called *punctiliar,* action, and can be illustrated this way:

• (a period)

The other denotes *durative* , or *linear* action, and can be illustrated this way:

______________ (a line)

(* The word "tense", meaning "time", is not an accurate description of the forms for Greek verbs. But because Greek grammarians have adopted the word, we use it in this grammar.)

Keep in mind, it is the ***action*** Greek verbs emphasize, rather than the time element.

You will find five *primary** tenses in most verbs in *New Testament* Greek.

To understand these tenses well, let us look at them more closely, and illustrate them in Bible Greek.

(1) **PRESENT TENSE (__________)**

The **present tense** is a continous, ongoing action, which makes it *linear*, or durative.

We illustrate its usage as a *line* **(_______).**

We find the **present tense** at 1 Timothy 3:14:

Ταῦτά	σοι	γράφω
These things	to you	**I [now] write.**

(*We will consider five basic Greek tenses in this grammar and add more to later studies.)

Note the *continuous* action of the verb *"I [now] write"*. It, therefore, would be translated into English as *"I am writing."*

Note: Verbs in the present tense that end with the Greek omega (ω) usually refer to the person, *"I"*. (See Rom. 3:5; Gal. 2:2)

The present tense is durative in quality and frequently refers to *linear action.*

(2) IMPERFECT TENSE (. . . . .)

Of all the tenses, the imperfect is the closest to expressing *time element*, although, the action is always *durative.*

It is difficult to translate the Greek **imperfect** into English, for the English does not have a parallel to the Greek.

At best, we can explain the function of the imperfect in terms *we* can understand; and this we will proceed to do.

As illustrated earlier, the **imperfect** tense is is shown like this: **. . . . .**

It is similar to the **present** tense in linear action, but it is like a motion picture, giving us frame by frame, *actions* being carried out.

Some of these may even be *past actions* bringing us into the present and creating a vivid scene that is carried *through* the present.

Let us look at a Bible example of this. Please turn to Matthew 3:4, which describes the preaching work of John the Baptist:

Ἰωάνης	*εἶχεν*	τὸ	ἔνδυμα	αὐτοῦ
John	**was having on** *(imperfect tense)*	the	garment	of him.

(Note: *εἶχεν* looks like the English past tense.)

But we must keep in focus: *durative action.*

We have described what John wore. That was the first frame of our cinema in motion. The second continues to unravel the story for us. Verse 5:

Τότε	ἐξεπορεύετο	πρὸς	αὐτὸν
Then	**were advancing out**	toward	him
	(Imperfect tense)		

The *action* of the people of Jerusalem and Judea is *"then"* pictured for us. They *'advanced'* toward John. And why? The **imperfect** continues at Vs. 6:

καὶ	ἐβαπτίζοντο . . .	ὑπ’	αὐτοῦ
and	**were undergoing baptism** . . .	by	him
	(Imperfect tense)		

Did you follow the series of events? The **imperfect** carries us through the course of the entire story, and toward a conclusion. We see history moving before us frame by frame. The **imperfect** is a flowing river current, leading us in the course of a whole event.

The **imperfect** tense can describe a ***series***, as demonstrated, or it can describe an ***act***.

Either description can be interpreted from
Mark 12:41:

καὶ	πολλοὶ	πλούσιοι	ἔβαλλον
and	many	wealthy men	**were casting** . . .
			(imperfect tense)

Did these wealthy men *'cast'* money into the treasury at one time, or was it a number of times?

In other places, it is clearly *repetition*. Acts 3:3:

ἠρώτα	ἐλεημοσύνην	λαβεῖν.
he was beseeching	gifts of compassion	to receive.
(imperfect tense)		

(See also Mark 7:26; John 4:31)

One important thing about the **imperfect** tense is evident: the action is either *attempted* or left *incomplete*. Even in a series, the end is not evident.

(3) AORIST TENSE (_____ . _____)

The name for the **aorist** tense means *undefined action.* (Greek, ἄοριστος, literally: *"no horizon"*).

At times, it appears to be a past tense, but the Greeks used it to mean a *single act* without consideration of time.

Unlike the imperfect which "describes", the **aorist** refers to *punctiliar*, or *momentary* action, each case viewed as a *whole.*

For example:

Romans 15:15

ἔγραψα	ὑμῖν	ἀπὸ	μέρους,
I wrote	to you	in	part,
(aorist tense)			

It ignores any *interval* between its *action* and, in this case, the *moment* Paul speaks about it.

The *aorist* is the most common tense used in Greek, but it is unique:

It draws no distinction between past, present, and future tenses, but keeps *single action* to the fore: For another example:

Romans 6:15

Τί	οὖν;	ἁμαρτήσωμεν . . . ;
What	therefore?	**Shall we sin . . . ?**
		(aorist subjunctive)

Here, Paul was asking: *"Should we commit a sin?"* (A single act without reference to time).

Notice, too, the Greek word is in the ***aorist*** *subjunctive. Subjunctive* denotes the *mood* of the verb, which we will discuss soon.

So, the aorist tense does not involve the time element, but the *point of action of the verb.*

Other examples are: John 5:8 ἆρον, *"take up your mat."*; Matt. 18:23 ὡμοιώθη, *"has become as. . ."*

4- FUTURE TENSE (_______ >)

The **future** tense in Greek carries a similar meaning as in English. (*"I will be going."*)

Focus, though, is on the kind of *action* rather than the *time* involved.

The **future** tense concentrates on action that *is pending,* that *which will take place.*

Notice *two* instances of its use at John 14:3:

ἑτοιμάσω τόπον ὑμῖν . . . καὶ
I must prepare place for you . . . and
(future tense)

παραλήμψομαι* . . .
I shall receive beside . . .
(future tense)

Here, "I must prepare" and *"I shall receive beside"* are *actions* which will take place in the future.

*The spelling of this Greek verb is according to two highly accurate Greek texts used by Bible scholars today.

Future action is especially evident in application of prophecy at Hebrews 8:10:

ἐπὶ καρδίας αὐτῶν ἐπιγράψω
upon hearts of them **I shall write deeply upon**
(future tense)

Observe above the **future** tense of γράφω ("*I [now] write*"). At 1 Tim. 3:14, we saw the **present** tense of this word; And at Rom. 15:15, we noted the **aorist** tense: ἔγραψα (*I wrote").*

Notice, also, the **stem** in all three words: γρα

As with nouns, verbs have a **stem**, that part of the word which *never changes*, but which identifies the word as belonging to the same family.

When you check your Greek interlinear at Hebrews 8:10, you will find three other **future** tenses in that verse. They are identified in the interlinear reading by the English words *"will"*, and *"shall."*

5- PERFECT TENSE (_________ .)

The **perfect** tense expresses a completed state with the results remaining.

We can think of a Greek Marathon runner who has completed his race. The action is accomplished, followed by an enduring effect.

The runner can say he has won the race, but also, that he is the winner. *(present **perfect**)*

So at 2 Tim. 4:7, the apostle Paul could say at the end of his Christian course:

τὸν	καλὸν	ἀγῶνα	ἠγώνισμαι,
the	gallant	struggle	**I have struggled,**

τὸν	δρόμον	τετέλεκα,
the	course	**I have completed,**

τὴν	πίστιν	τετήρηκα·
the	faith	**I have maintained;**

This example gives us three **perfects.** Paul has successfully endured to the end of his life, and, like the runner, looks back at his arduous course with a full sense of satisfaction.

In a similar way, when we disclose that our mission has been accomplished, we say "the job is done."

Let us use our example of the word "*write*." The form of this word in the **perfect** tense is found at John 19:22. Pontius Pilate said:

Ὃ	γέγραφα,	γέγραφα.
What	**I have written,**	**I have written.**

Pilate told the chief priests he had finished his work, and he was not going to change it. It was staying that way. Looking back, he was satisfied.

This reveals the sense of the **perfect** tense, as shown by the illustration: _________ **.** Linear and punctiliar ideas are combined. That is, course and effect are seen together.

To *grasp clearly* the **action** of the tenses we have considered, let us look at them together:

The Present Tense *continues, is on-going;*

(__________)

The Imperfect Tense *describes a series, or attempted, or uncompleted action;*

(. . . . .)

The Aorist Tense *considers a single, completed act during an undefined period;*

(_____ . ______)

The Future Tense *refers to pending action;*

(_________ >)

The Perfect Tense *is completed action.*

(__________ .)

B. CONJUGATION OF VERBS

When we discussed nouns, we explained their changes as **declensions**, or inflections.

When verbs are changed, we call this **conjugation.**

A verb is conjugated to give its *voices, moods, tenses, numbers,* and *persons* in their proper order.

We have already explained **tenses**, so let us look at the other parts of the verb:

1- **VOICES -** Greek verbs have *three voices:*

(a) **active**, (b) **passive**, and (c) **middle**.

(a) The ***active*** voice shows the subject *doing* or *being* something, such as:

John 1:26

Ἐγὼ βαπτίζω, ***"I am baptizing."***

Subject **Active Verb**

(b) The ***passive*** voice shows something *being done to,* or *for* the subject, such as:

John 1:17

ὁ νόμος	διὰ	Μωυσέως	ἐδόθη,
the law	*through*	*Moses*	***was given,***
Subject			**Passive Verb**

(c) The ***middle*** voice shows the subject doing something to *itself,* or for *itself,* such as:

Matthew 27:5

ἀπήγξατο.

he hanged himself.

Subject and Verb Combined

2- **MOODS** - There are *four* moods:

(α) The **indicative**, which gives a mere statement of fact, as Ἐγένετο ἄνθρωπος, *"There came forth a man."* (John 1:6);

(β) The **imperative**, which gives a command or exhortation, as Γεμίσατε, *"Fill (you) [the water jars.]"* (John 2:7) (γ) The **subjunctive**, where a possibility is suggested, as in ἁμαρτίας ᾖ πεποιηκώς, *"he **may** have engaged in sins."* James 5:15;

(δ) The **optative,** which expresses a wish, as γένοιτό μοι, *"May it come to pass with me."* Luke 1:38;

(ε) The **infinitive**, which we place here, has been thought to be a mood, but is, in reality, a *verba noun*, retaining the functions of noun and verb.

For example, look at Mark 5:43:

δοθῆναι	αὐτῇ	φαγεῖν.
to be provided *(infinitive)*	to her	to eat

Note the action of the verb in the phrase *"to be provided"* while the subject, or noun is not mentioned, but is understood.

This is a unique form of Greek grammar which will be considered in later studies.

3- NUMBER AND PERSON-

Other parts of the verb which are changed involve the ***number*** of persons spoken to or about (plural or singular), and . . .

person, whether *first person*, such as "I believe," *second person*, "you believe," or *third person*, "he, she, or they believe."

A Greek translator must have all the foregoing parts of the verb correctly in mind so he can properly translate the verb.

A *lexicon* containing all the schematics of a word will break down the verb for you to show its voice, tense, mood, number, and person.

Ex: πίστευσον *"(You) manifest faith."*

(LUKE 8:50)

Each part of the word tells the trained eye the way the different parts of the verb are to be translated.

Here is how the word and its description might look like in your notebook after your research:

πί σ τευ·σον
pi' stev- son *(transliteration ours)*

2 per[son] sing[ular] aor[ist] 1, im[perative]

To help you see clearly their individual components, we'll list the parts of the verb:

person	*number*	*tense*	*mood*	*voice*
2nd (you)	singular	1st aorist	imperative	active

So, in the above example, πίστευσον, "*you* (singular) *believe*," we note action is required by the subject *(imperative mood, active voice)*. Since his decision is dependent on his response, the verb is indefinite in reference to time *(aorist)*. It is also in the second person (you). Hence, the command: **"Believe (**or, **manifest faith)."**

Of course, there are many other forms of the words *"have faith"* (or *"believe"*) in Greek, and your grammatical lexicon lists all of them for you as they appear in the *"New Testament."*

Look in your lexicon under **πιστεύω** ("pis-tev' o, *I believe* "). Here, you will observe this verb in it many forms as it defines tense, mood, voice, number and person.

First, identify the **verb-stem**, the part of the verb that never changes.

Using our example, the stem of **πίστευσον** is **πιστε,** as your lexicon heading may note.

Sometimes it is the letters *before* the **stem**, or those *after* the **stem** which give you the clue regarding its use as to tense, mood, etc. Your lexicon will acquaint you with these many *conjugations* of the verb.

As you use your Greek, you will be able to spot each part of the verb which tells you its proper form.

To assist you to effectively use a lexicon, let us look at some of the various forms of the verb πιστεύω:

At **John 4:21**, we find the form πίστευέ, (*"Be believing"*), which is: second person singular present imperative. (Jesus is speaking with the Samaritan woman with an imperative appeal)

Another form is found at **John 12:44**, πιστεύει, (*"is believing"*), third person, singular present indicative, continuous action.

A third can be seen at **Luke 24:25**, πιστεύειν, (*"to be believing"*). This is present infinitive.

The fourth, πιστεύεις, (*"are you believing?"*) can be viewed at **John 1:50**. This is second person singular present indicative.

A fifth form, πιστεύεται, (*"is being believed"*) is observed at **Romans 10:10**.(Third person singular present indicative passive)

Another form, a sixth, is located at **John 3:12,** πιστεύετε, (*"you are believing"*). It is second person plural present indicative imperative mood. It is noted here with the negative particle "not.

A final form is gleaned from **John 13:19,** πιστεύητε, (*"you could be believing"*) The form is second person plural present subjuntive mood. Here, Jesus addresses believers.

All the above are forms of the word πιστεύω, *"I believe."*

"THEOU" REVIEW 2

1- **Why did the Greeks use the article *"ho"*?** **(Answer- pp. 37, 38)**

2- **What happens to the definite article when a noun is declined, and why?** **(Answer- p. 38)**

3- **Give two reasons for the article's absence in Greek?** **(Answer- pp. 41-43)**

4- **Why do translators properly add "a" or "an" before a noun in some instances, though not in the Greek?** **(Answer- pp. 44, 45)**

5- **What do Greek verb tenses describe, and what two verb-types do we find in Greek?** **(Answer- p. 46)**

6- **Name the *five primary tenses* and their *symbols*.** **(Answer- pp. 47, 48)**

7- **Which tense denotes *completed action*?** **(Answer- pp. 48, 57-8)**

8- **Which tense means *undefined action*?** **(Answer- pp. 47, 53-4)**

9- **Identify the tense which describes a *series*, or shows *uncompleted action*?** **(Answer- pp. 47, 49-52)**

10- **Give the tense showing *continuous action*.** **(Answer- pp. 47-9)**

11- **Name the *three voices*, the *four moods*, and the verbal-noun.** **(Answer- pp. 60-62)**

Let us pause for a moment and reflect on our studies of Greek.

We hope the *manner* in which you are learning Greek is tantalizing to your mental taste buds. Are the illustrations helping you?

If you are having some difficulty understanding everything, do not be dismayed. Many who have begun this course have not grasped all things at once. It takes repetition. It takes meditation, and it requires balance. Do not flood your mind with everything at once.

Greek is like eating food which requires much "chewing", and "digesting." It is not a subject one can gobble down.

So, reflect on what you've learned, and be satisfied with your progress. You may have to go over these chapters again and again, but you *will* learn. It is your desire that counts.

Well, shall we proceed with our lessons?

CHAPTER 7

PREPOSITIONS

Prepositions are *indeclinable words* which express relations of nouns to other words in the sentence;

Though the ***cases*** may show the relation of nouns to other words, ***prepositions*** are there to express greater *emphasis*.

To make our study more enjoyable, we are going to imagine Greek prepositions are *people*.

I would like to introduce to you:

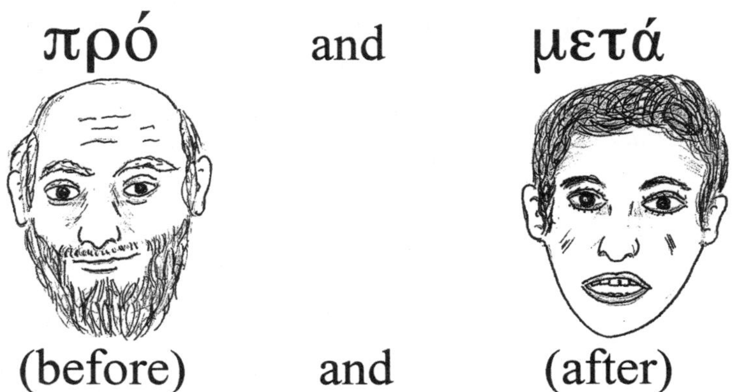

πρό ("pro") is always early and μετά ("meta") is always late. **πρό** is elderly, and μετά, young.

English has adopted these Greek terms, as in **pro**logue, an introduction to (or what comes **before**) a play; and **meta**morphosis, (a change of form, or what comes **after** the change.)

1- We see **πρό** in Matthew 11:10:

ἐγὼ ἀποστέλλω τὸν ἄγγελόν*
I am sending the messenger

μου **πρὸ** προσώπου σου
of me **before** face of you.

2- We also see μετά in Matthew 27:63:

Μετὰ τρεῖς ἡμέρας ἐγείρομαι·
After three days I am being raised [to life].

So remember our friends πρό and μετά who come *before* and *after* each other.

(* *angelon,* "angel." When one gamma follows another, it is given a nasal sound, as in the English word "angle.")

I would also like to introduce to you:

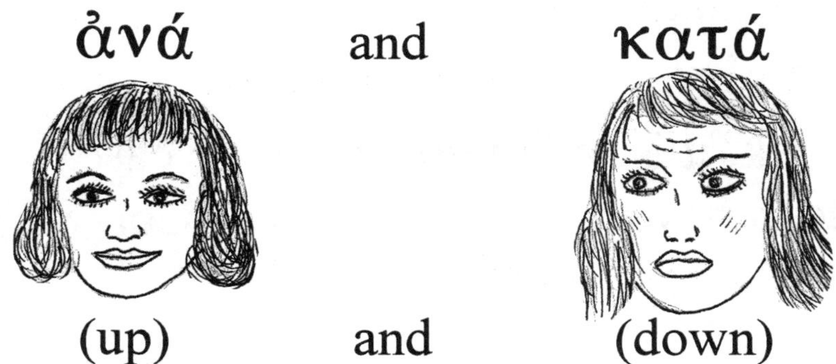

ἀνά ("ana") is frequently happy, while κατά ("kata") is often sullen.

English uses these words as prefixes for its own words. For instance, "***ana***batic" refers to rising wind currents, meaning "to go **up,**" from the Greek ἀνά.

The same is true in Greek. ἀνά is usually prefixed to verbs, signifying the preposition **"up"**, as at Luke 5:19:

ἀναβάντες	ἐπὶ	τὸ	δῶμα
having stepped **up**	upon	the	roof.

The prefix κατά forms the beginning of the English word "**cata**strophe," which means, "to set **down**."

In Greek, it is seen in the genitive case describing the deep poverty of Christians (2 Cor. 8:2):

καὶ	ἡ	κατὰ	βάθους	πτωχέια
and	the	down	deepgoing	poverty

(Observe the vivid language of the Greek.)

κατά is also often used as a prefix in Greek words as καταβας ("having arrived **down**") at Luke 6:17. (Also John 5:7; Acts 10:11)

The prepositions κατά and ανά have other meanings, but they *basically* refer to "up" and "down".

A good way to remember these two prepositions is that the one (ανά) is always **"up"** and happy, and the other (κατά) is **"down"** and sad.

Two other Greek "individuals," who are close relatives, come to meet us:

Both are named ἐπί

ἐπί
(upon)

ἐπί
(over)

Why does the same Greek word have different meanings?

The first ἐπί describes the *basic* meaning of the preposition ("upon"), while the second ἐπί refers to the subject *exercising power*, or *authority,* as in the case of a king ruling "over" something or someone.

That is why we picture the second ἐπί as wearing a *crown*.

It is not difficult to see these different uses of ἐπί in the Christian Greek Scriptures.

1- For instance, the first ἐπί is seen at Matthew 9:2, which denotes *place*:

παραλυτικὸν ἐπὶ κλίνης
a paralytic **upon** bed.

(See also Matt. 6:10; 14:25; 24:17; Rev. 5:13)

2- The second ἐπί, denoting *authority*, is observed at Revelation 9:11:

ἔχουσιν ἐπ᾽ αὐτῶν βασιλέα
They are having **over*** them a king.

*(*While Greek interlinears often render ἐπί as "upon," the student must understand that this is the* ***basic*** *meaning of the word. It is clear from the context here that ἐπί carries the sense as "over," and is to be translated to convey authority. See Eph. 4:6; Rev. 13:7; 16:9; 17:18)*

(*Note*: When some prepositions come before a word beginning with a vowel, they drop the last letter. In this case ἐπί becomes ἐπ᾽ because it precedes **αὐτῶν,** which begins with a vowel. This rule is called *elision*. We will cover more of this in later studies.)

Please do not be overwhelmed by all these "people" prepositions. You will come to know them well as you use the Koine Greek.

Let us introduce to you a beautiful woman named δıά and her jealous sister περί.

δıά (through)

περί (about)

δıά gets **through** to people, while περί goes **about** getting approval in wrong ways.

English uses δıά in words like "**dia**meter", meaning "a straight line **through** the center of a figure."

περί has usage in English words like "**peri**meter" which describes the boundary **around** an area.

It is also *easy* to see these usages in Greek.

1- Regarding διά, we read at Matthew 2:12:

δι'	ἄλλης	ὁδοῦ	ἀνεχώρησαν
through	another	road	they departed

2- Regarding περί, we observe at Matthew 3:4:

δερματίνην	περὶ	τὴν	ὀσφὺν	αὐτοῦ
leathern	**around**	the	hip (loin)	of him

Greek expression incorporates these prepositions as *prefixes* to words, such as: διάκονος, which describes a minister, and which literally means "*through* the dust." (1 Timothy 4:6)

And: περιεβλέπετο, which means "he was looking **around**." (Mark 5:32)

You will discover that many of the prepositions we have considered, and those we will briefly mention, use prepositions in *compound words*.

Here are some other *preposition* "people":

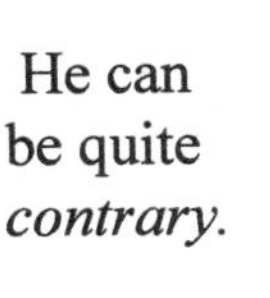

ἀντί

"instead of," "against"

(Luke 11:11)

"I am the father of many. They come *from* me."

ἀπό

"from"

(Luke 22:41-43)

She is prone to getting *into* other people's business.

ἐν (εἰς)

"in"; "entering"

(Matt. 1:18; John 3:22)

These two brothers seek to get *out of* everything.

ἐκ, ἐξ ***(before vowel)***

"out of"

(Matt. 8:28; Luke 1:78)

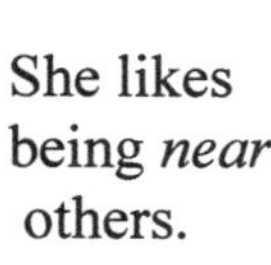

παρά

"beside," "near"

(John 19:25)

He is known as one who works *toward* his goals.

πρός

("to, toward")

(John 11:15)

She is quite haughty and feels she is *above* others.

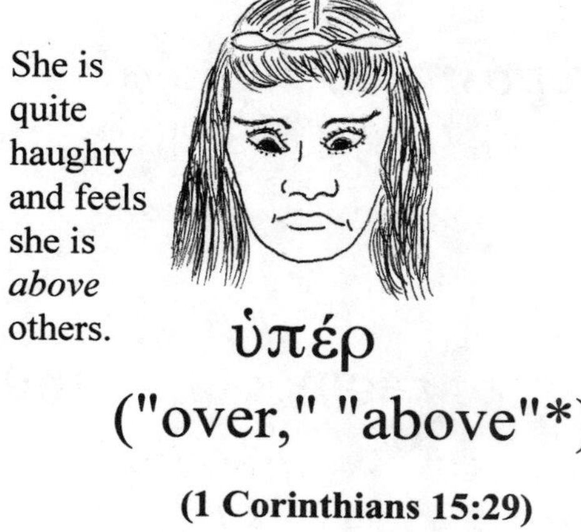

ὑπέρ
("over," "above"*)

(1 Corinthians 15:29)

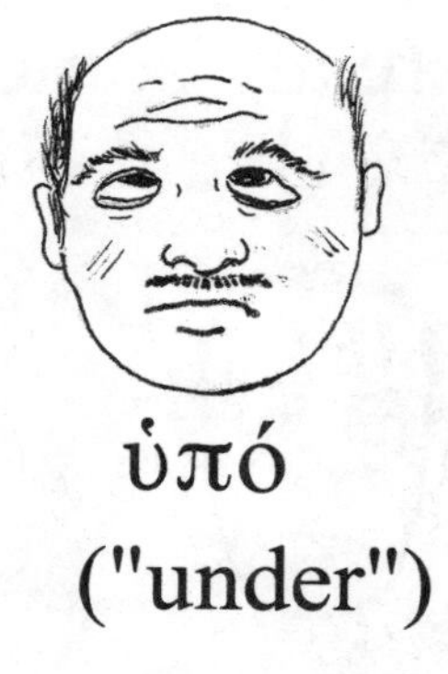

He has low self-esteem and views himself as *beneath* others.

ὑπό
("under")

(Matthew 5:15)

(* ὑπέρ does not appear by itself in the "New Testament" to denote *place*, although it is seen in *compound* words as at Hebrews 9:5, ὑπεράνω ("up above"); and Acts 1:13, ὑπερῷον ("upper room"). On its own, ὑπέρ conveys the idea of being 'about,' or 'concerning' someone or thing, such as something done 'on behalf of' the subject.

Greek prepositions are often seen at the *beginning* of compound words. They will assist you to identify those words, as in the examples noted above.

Learn to break down the word by distinguishing the preposition. Then sound out each following syllable, and you will master that word.

There are other *preposition* "folks" you will meet in your Greek interlinear. They will assist you in understanding important phrases in the Greek text. Study each one carefully and try to remember them by the *personalities* we have given each one.

CHAPTER 8

ADJECTIVES, ADVERBS, AND PARTICIPLES

A) ADJECTIVES

How often we have characterized someone or thing as *"beautiful," "nice," "great,"* or *"wonderful!"*

Greek ***adjectives***, as those in English, describe the nature or function of a noun or pronoun.

Hebrews 9:4 gives a vivid picture of the χρυσοῦν θυμιατήριον, the "*golden* censer" in the Most Holy.

John 4:11 informs us the well from which the Samaritan woman drew water for Jesus was βαθύ, "*deep*." No wonder he used this water as an illustration of the life-giving *"water"* he offered her.

At Matthew 5:36, Jesus contrasts λευκήν, "*white*" hair from μέλαιναν, "*black*", impressing upon us that once a vow is made, it cannot be changed.

We see the value of *adjectives* as they draw a vivid picture of what the Greek text teaches us.

Adjectives can be either *attributive*, or *predicative* (part of a predicate).

1- ***Attributive-*** This kind of adjective qualifies *(describes)* the noun, as in "the *wise* man."

"They **attribute** to me great *wisdo*
Well, if they must ."

2- ***Predicative-*** This kind of adjective makes the above statement in the form of a *predicate,* as in "the man is *wise.*" (A *predicate* makes a statement about the subject).

The **predicative** adjective can *precede* the noun (and include the article), or *follow* the noun and not take the article. Let's use the above example:

σοφὸς	ὁ	ἀνήρ,	**or**	ὁ	ἀνὴρ	σοφός
wise	the	man,	**or**	the	man	**wise.**

We're taking time to explain this, because you will often see that Greek uses a word-order* different from that of English.

* The order in which Greek writers placed words in a sentence or phrase..

B) ADVERBS

English *adverbs* describe time, manner, degree, cause, etc. of a verb. So does Greek.

As English words use a suffix to modify a *verb,* i.e., adding "ly" to "quick" to form "quick**ly**", so Greek changes the final form of words to make them adverbs.

Ex: δικαίος, "righteous (one)"; (adjective)
δικαίως, "righteous**ly**"; (adverb)

Adverbs are often viewed as unimportant, but they form a large part of Greek grammar.

As an example of the adverb in the accusative case, we can look at Matthew 10:8:

δωρεὰν	ἐλάβετε
free(ly)	you received
adverb	*verb*

(See also Matt. 5:25, ταχὺ, "quickly").

C) PARTICIPLES

*"Don't let the one hump fool you. I'm **verb** and adjective **combined.**"*

Participles are *verbal adjectives.* They agree with the noun in gender, number, and case.

*"Call me τέος. I'm both **verb** and **adjective.**"*

Those ending in τέος are used to indicate *necessity*, as at Luke 5:38:

εἰς ἀσκοὺς καινοὺς βλητέον*
into leathern bags new (ones) *to be pitched.*

[*The accusative form of βλητέος.]

(Note: βλητέον, *"to be pitched,"* is like a verb in action, but describes as an adjective.)

The participle ending in τός is seen in this expression at Matthew 3:17:

*"I'm τός. I am **verb** and **adjective** also.*

ὁ υἱός μου ὁ ἀγαπητός
the son of me the *beloved (one).*

(Note: The Son is the *"beloved (one)"* He is *loved* by his Father [verb], whom the Father describes in *affectionate terms* [adjective]).

As noted, not all participles end in τέος, but they always are both *adjective* and *verb.*

An interesting use of the participle **τός** is found at Luke 9:62 where a disciple who looks behind is **not** . . .
εὔθετός ἐστιν τῇ βασιλείᾳ τοῦ θεοῦ.
well-suited is to the kingdom of the God.

(Note: The term *"well-suited"* is a participle defining the person's spiritual status.)

Other forms are noted at Ephesians 4:28, ὁ κλέπτων, *"the thief"* (or *"stealer"*), and at Matthew 5:22, ὁ ὀργιζόμενος, "*the (one) being angry*." Verb and adjective are combined.

The present participle describes linear action and can be used with a verb in various tenses. (Matt. 6:27; Mark 3:31; John 9:25; Acts 4:34.)

The participle is used freely in Greek, and most of its uses can easily be translated into English.

Participles in Greek fall into a number of **catagories.** Here are two more examples:

1- The Attributive Participle- It is used to qualify a noun nearly the same way as an attributive adjective, but the *participle* generally refers to some **definite known instance,** as at 1 Peter 5:10:

*"It was definitely at **that** time."*

Ὁ . . θεὸς . . ὁ καλέσας. . .ὀλίγον παθόντας
the God . . **the [one] having called. . .** little [while] [ones] having felt pain

Here, καλέσας* refers to *a definite known act* of calling, but παθόντας to general suffering.

*(*In this scripture, this participle is nominative singular masculine aorist active)*

2- Circumstantial Participle- It expresses *certain relations* of time, place, cause, means, manner, purpose, or condition.

*"I know the **circumstances** involved."*

The *temporal idea* of "having stood up", is seen at Matt. 26:62; *the cause of an act,* "nothing finding," at Acts 4:21; *the means,* "lyingly say,"at Matt. 5:11; *the manner,* at Luke 1:64.

CHAPTER 9

PRONOUNS

In your study of Greek, you will identify more valuable pearls- the various *pronouns* in Greek.

1- Personal Pronouns- ἐγώ (English- "e·go' "), meaning "I"; σύ, meaning "you"; and their plurals ἡμεῖς, "we"; and ὑμεῖς, "you" (more than one), are only used in the *nominative case.*

This is true when special stress is laid on the person mentioned, or in *apposition** to proper names.

(**Apposition* means the placing of a word or expression beside another so that the second explains, and has the same grammatical construction as the first. Ex: "John, *my brother*, is here.")

Of course, personal pronouns are declined, according to case, so that ἐγώ in the *nominative* becomes ἐμέ or μέ in the *accusative* case; ἐμοῦ or μοῦ in the *genitive* case, as noted in your lexicon.

The personal pronoun αὐτός always means "himself" in the nominative case (John 2:24;16:27).

αὐτός is expressed emphatically as "he" when translated into English at such places as Matt. 1:21: ("for *he* will save his people."), Matt. 8:24: ("but *he* was sleeping."), and Mark 1:8: (but *he* will baptize you . . .").

In what are called the *oblique* cases (accusative, genitive, dative), the pronoun may simply be used as the personal pronoun of the *third person*, meaning, *him* (Matt. 4:10); *her* (John 11:33); and *it* (Matt. 5:29) .

"This is ***my [ἐμός]*** *moment."*

2- **Possessive Pronoun-** This pronoun names who or what *has* something.

The possessive pronoun ἐμός, "my," can be seen in its declined forms at John 4:34: ("my food is ..."), and John 15:11: ("my joy"). The possessive pronoun σός, "your," (*σοῦ, genitive singular*) can be noted three times at Matt. 7:4.

The possessive pronoun ἡμέτερος, **our** is observed at Acts 2:11: ("in **our** tongues.") and Acts 26:5: ("**our** form of worship").

The possessive pronoun ὑμέτερος,* **your**, literally- **"yours"**(plural), can be seen at John 8:17: ("in **your** (plural) own law . . ."), and at Gal. 6:13: ("boasting in **your** (plural) flesh.")
(ὑμέτερος differs from ἡμέτερος as noted by the first letter of each word, but are declined the same.)*

3- Reciprocal Pronouns- These pronouns express mutual action or relation. In English, we say: "as," and "each other," etc.

In Greek, the reciprocal pronoun ἀλλήλους ("*one another*") is declined regularly in its forms in the plural (ἀλλήλας, ἀλλήλα); it has no singular form.

We see ἀλλήλους at 1 Cor. 16:20: ("Greet *one another.*"); also at 1 John 4:7: ("continue loving *one another.*"); and at Matt. 24:10: ("will betray . . . and hate *one another.*").

4- **Reflexive Pronoun-** The pronoun that is used as a direct object of a verb, as in "I help *myself.*"

"At times, I must ***reflect*** *on* ***myself."***

In the first person, Greek uses ἐμαυτὸν, "*myself,*" at Matt. 8:9: ("having authority under *myself.*"); Gal. 2:18: ("I demonstrate *myself* to be a transgressor.")

In the second person, the Greek gives σεαυτοῦ, "*yourself,*" at John 8:13: ("you bear witness about *yourself.*"); Acts 16:28: ("do not hurt *yourself.*") (See also Romans 2:5)

In the third person, Greek shows ἑαυτοῦ, "*himself,*" at Matt. 27:42: ("*himself* he cannot save."); "*itself,*" at Rom. 14:14: ("nothing is defiled in *itself.*")

5- **Demonstrative Pronouns-** This pronoun is so named because it points out, as in the words "this" and "that."

Greek *demonstrative* pronouns are:

(a) οὗτος and ὅδε - "*this, (or, "this one").*

(Note: Both words are aspirated; thus transliterated "hou' tos'" and "ho' de.")

οὗτος is found at Matt. 3:17: ("*This* is my Son.") (See also John 1:15, 30)

ὅδε appears at James 4:13 combined with the definite article: (*"to this city,"* Greek- *τήνδε*)

(b) ἐκεῖνος - *"that," (or, "that one").*

ἐκεῖνος means "*that*" man, woman, or thing. The word generally refers to someone or thing *more remote* than the others.

For example, at Luke 18:14: "*This* man (Gr- οὗτος) . . . proved more righteous than *that* (Gr- ἐκεῖνος) man."

"This** is **'hou'tos,"** and **that** is **'e-kei'nos.'"

(Note the contrast: The former is *near,* while the latter is *more remote.*)

We note ἐκεῖνος applied to Moses at John 5:46; ἐκείνου (genitive case) to Jesus at Acts 3:13; ἐκείνοις (plural) to unbelievers at Mark 4:11; ἐκείνη (feminine gender) to the old law covenant at Hebrews 8:7, and to a house at Matt. 7:25, 27.

As you can see, ἐκεῖνος in its many forms or declensions can refer either to persons or to impersonal things, called *"grammatical gender."*

Grammatical gender developed from natural gender distinctions by means of the Greek habit of personalizing inanimate things. (*The Greeks made most rivers, months, and winds masculine; A majority of towns, countries and islands are feminine, as are some qualities and actions*).

The *Koine* Greek embraced the use of grammatical gender and writers of the *"New Testament"* employed the practice extensively in the sacred Greek text.

Note the grammatical use of gender and personality with reference to ἐκεῖναί at John 5:39.

Here, Jesus points to the *Holy Scriptures*, and says:

ἐκεῖναί	εἶσιν	αἱ	μαρτυροῦσαι
those	are	the (ones)	bearing witness
feminine plural			

περὶ	ἐμοῦ·
about	me;

Observe the "personality" of the Scriptures that is expressed in Greek grammar. To learn Greek, we must *think* Greek, and not hastily attach English or other language interpretations to our studies.

Let us consider another example: Referring to the *word* Jesus speaks which will judge his listeners, he states, at John 12:48:

ἐκεῖνος	κρινεῖ	αὐτὸν
that (one)	will judge	him
masculine gender		

Your studies of pronouns and other parts of speech will examine words that are personalized. The cautious student will be careful to distinguish between what subjects are truly personal and those which are merely so described grammatically.

6- **Relative Pronouns-** This pronoun introduces a subordinate clause and refers to an antecedent.* (Ex: "The book *which* you bought.")

(* ***antecedent***- *A word, or phrase, to which a pronoun refers. In the above case, the phrase "the book" is the antecedent.)*

*"How about: **'the donkey wh** you bought? (hint, hint).'"*

The relative pronouns ὅς *("who," "which")*, and ὅστις *("who[what]ever"),* are declined in various ways, and agree with the *antecedent* in gender and number, as in the feminine of ὅς:

Example: (Acts 3:25)

καὶ	τῆς	διαθήκης	ἧς	ὁ	θεὸς
and	of the	covenant	***which***	the	God . . .
		(antecedent)	*(relative pronoun)*		

Note how διαθήκης ("covenant"), and ἧς (*"which"*) agree in gender and number. Both are in the singular number and feminine gender, as well as in the genitive case.

Another example is seen at 1 Corinthians 10:16:

τὸν	ἄρτον	ὅν	κλῶμεν
the	thin loaf	**which**	we are breaking.
	(antecedent)	*(relative pronoun)*	

Again, observe how the antecedent and relative pronoun agree in number, gender, and case. Here, they are in the singular number, masculine gender, and accusative case.

Other *kinds* of pronouns seen in Greek are:

7- **Interrogative Pronouns,** forms of τίς ("who," "which," and "what"), as at Matt. 3:7; 27:17 and Acts 13:25), which are used to form questions.

8- **Indefinite Pronouns**- In these instances, τις takes on another role, that of an *enclitic**, and means "anybody" or "anyone," as at Matthew 11:27; or "someone" (τινα) at Acts 5:36. Note that the enclitic pronoun has no accent.

*(***enclitic-** a word that leans on a preceding word for accent.)*

9- **Negative Pronouns-** Οὐδείς *("No one")* is the most common negative pronoun.

It is seen at Matthew 6:24: *"No one (οὐδείς) can slave for two masters."* (Also Acts 4:12).

μηδείς is another negative pronoun that means *"no one,"* but is not as frequent as οὐδείς. It is found at 1 Cor. 3:18,21; Gal. 6:17; Jas. 1:13.

An unusual negative pronoun is οὐ πᾶς and means: *"not everyone,"* as noted in Jesus' words at Matt. 7:21.

Negative Particles

*"Please do not think **negatively** of me."*

This seems a good place to mention these since they are used in a similar way as negative pronouns.

There are two negative particles in Greek, οὐ and μή.

Negative Particles (cont'd)

οὐ is *objective*, while μή is *subjective*. What does this mean?

οὐ denies facts; it is direct and positive; μή is more doubtful and subtle as it denies thoughts and concepts.

"No way!" *"Well . . . maybe not."*

For example, οἳ οὐ πιστεύουσιν, *"you that do **not** believe"* (John 6:64), is a definite fact, offering little hope, whereas ἔργα δὲ μὴ ἔχῃ, *"but he does **not** have works"* (James 2:14), is conditional, depending on action.

The expanded form οὐχί emphasized the negative οὐ as seen at Luke 1:60: *"**No (Οὐχί)**, indeed! but (ἀλλὰ) he shall be called John."*

Note how ἀλλὰ sets the negative particle in sharp contrast to his statement.
There are numerous compound words which begin with the negative particles οὐ and μή. You will enjoy using them as you pursue Greek.

"THEOU" REVIEW 3

1- Which prepositions describe *"before"* and *"after"*?
(Answer- p. 12)

2- Does ἐπί always mean *"upon"*? Explain. **(Ans- pp. 73,74)**

3- How will prepositions help to identify some words?
(Answer- p. 78)

4- What are the two kinds of adjectives, and what are their functions? **(Answer- p. 80)**

5- Give examples of adverbs in the Greek text. **(Ans- p. 81)**

6- What are participles and how useful are they in Greek?
(Answer- pp. 82-84)

7- Name four kinds of pronouns. **(Answer- pp. 85-94)**

8- Why are some pronouns personalized, even when they refer to impersonal things? **(Answer- pp. 90, 91)**

How did you fare with this review? If you have taken the time to study all three *"Theou Reviews"* and the material they are based on, it is clear you have a fundamental understanding of *Koine* Greek.

This does not mean you are a Greek scholar, but, an *informed student*. You can now proceed with the next, and most exciting, step- translation!

CHAPTER 10

PUTTING IT ALL TOGETHER: LET'S TRANSLATE!

How do you feel as you consider this title? A bit apprehensive? There is no need to feel this way. You have in your possession the right tools to dive into this ocean, and you have been building up your stamina by becoming familiar with the essential points of Greek grammar.

You are able to dive to great depths, and your pearls are within reach. Yes, you will have to proceed with caution, but now, all you have to do is to apply your training, and you *will* reach your goal. Let's do it together, and you will see how *natural* it is.

Remember: Before you begin, you must have the right tools. Do you have them before you?

1- **A Greek Interlinear**, which gives the literal word-for-word translation into English.

2- **A Greek Lexicon,** which presents all the words in the Greek in their various forms.

3- **A Notebook,** where you can write out for yourself the translation you will be composing.

As a translator, you will concern yourself with two branches of grammar: ***Accidence*** and ***Syntax***.

Accidence is the branch of study that examines the *forms* words take, or their *inflections,* in relation to other words. (For example, the different *cases* of the word θεός, and the varied forms of *verb tenses*).

Syntax is that branch of our study which centers on the *meaning* of these changes, their function, and how words are *arranged in a sentence.* It goes farther than accidence, as it considers the original meaning of each *word*, the accuracyof every *inflection,* and its scripture *context*.

So, using Accidence and Syntax, let us begin our translating.

*"O.K., **Accidence** has to do with the inflection of words, while **Syntax** deals with the arrangement of words in a sentence, and their meaning."*

Turn your Greek interlinear to John 20:31. Note the following clause in that verse:

Ἰησοῦς ἐστὶν* ὁ χριστὸς

(*ἐστὶν has the accent for emphasis when it is preceded by ὅτι ("that"), as seen earlier in this verse.)

The first step is to translate each word. Let's do it together:

Ἰησοῦς - "Jesus", nominative case

ἐστὶν - "is", verb, present tense, indicative mood

ὁ - "the", definite article, masculine

χριστὸς - "Christ," masculine gender.

So, the translation should be: *"Jesus is the Christ."*

To help you pronounce the Greek words, you may wish to *transliterate* each one, sounding out the Greek letters in English, as follows:

"Yee-soos' es-teen' ho Khrees-tos'. "

What we have just accomplished is ***Accidence***, the *study of words* and the *forms* they take in a sentence.

Now, using our above example, let's use ***Syntax***, and examine their *function* and the *arrangement* of these words in the sentence.

Here, the apostle John is making a statement about someone. So, grammatically, "Jesus" is the *subject,* and the clause, "is the Christ," is the *predicate*. Each sentence must have subject and predicate.

Ἰησοῦς	ἐστὶν	ὁ	χριστὸς
Jesus	is	the	Christ
[Subject]		*[Predicate]*	

To put it simply, the Subject is the *person or thing* speaking or spoken about, and the Predicate is *what is said* about the subject.

Note: The word-order in the Greek is the same here as in English. But in many cases, the verb or predicate *precedes* the subject.

It is common to see the following word-order in the Greek text: (John 12:36)

Ταῦτα	ἐλάλησεν	Ἰησοῦς
These (things)	spoke	Jesus
[Predicate]		*[Subject]*

(See also Matt. 13:34; Mark 14:72; John 10:6; 17:1)

It is clear that the word-order is changed and the subject is placed first when translating these verses into English. Example:

From: *"a demon you possess"* to *"You possess a demon." - John 7:20* *(See Page 43)*

Let us return to our example found at **John 20:31** in order to look closely at other points important to our translation.

In the phrase Ἰησοῦς ἐστὶν ὁ χριστὸς, "Jesus is the Christ," observe that the *iota* in Ἰησοῦς, and the *epsilon* in ἐστίν, are *unaspirated,* and therefore, would be transliterated without a beginning *"h"* sound.

However, when transliterating the omicron, ὁ, the article is *aspirated*, and would be given the sound *"ho."* ("the," nominative case, masculine gender).

All words agree regarding person, number, case and gender. Are you recalling some earlier points we learned?

Another important aspect of translation is finding the *definitions* to words you have translated.

For instance, do you know the definition of the name *Jesus*? Bible lexicons state Ἰησοῦς is the Greek form of the Hebrew name *Joshua*, and, according to several Greek lexicons and dictionaries, means "whose help (or salvation) is Jehovah."

The name *"Christ"* means "*anointed (one)*," and is the Greek equivalent of the Hebrew *"Messiah."* Jesus himself uses a verb-form of this word at Luke 4:18, when he said: "he [God] *anointed* (Gr-ἔχρισέν, ***"e-khri-sen"***) me to declare good news to the poor."

If you have not yet done so, you will find it helpful to acquire a *Greek-English lexicon* at your earliest convenience. This grammar will give you the definition of each word, its root, and its particular shade of meaning in its own context.

For more translating, let us return to John 20:31; Following the phrase we translated, there is another, which ties in well with the first. Note:

..... ὁ υἱὸς τοῦ θεοῦ,

Using our Greek-English lexicon, let's translate each word of this phrase:

ὁ	-	"the" (definite article, nominative case)
υἱὸς	-	"Son" (nominative case)
τοῦ	-	"of the," (genitive case)
θεοῦ	-	"God," (genitive case)

Observe in this phrase the agreement in case and gender of ὁ ("ho," *the*) with υἱὸς ("yos," *Son*), and τοῦ ("too," *of the*) with θεοῦ ("The-oo,'" *God*).

Did you also discover that this phrase is in *appositio*[n] to the previous phrase? Yes. The expression *"the Son of God"* is placed **beside** *"Jesus is the Christ,"* to show the relationship between the expressions, for υἱός and χριστός are both in the nominative case.

Now, on your own, go ahead and complete your translation of John 20:31. As you look in your Greek interlinear, you will see the Greek text as follows:

καὶ ἵνα πιστεύοντες ζωὴν ἔχητε ἐν τῷ ὀνόματι αὐτοῦ·

Keep in mind, *you* will be doing the translating. You will see under each Greek word in your interlinear, an English word which is provided by the interlinear's translator. Do not assume the definition is correct. It likely is, but check your Greek-English lexicon to prove it to yourself.

When translating, you will need to follow **two steps:**

1- Translate the word or phrase *directly from* the Greek into English.

2- Translate the correct *meaning* of the word and phrase from your English translation of the literal Greek.

For example, we translated: Ἰησοῦς ἐστὶν ὁ χριστὸς, ὁ υἱὸς τοῦ θεοῦ, which, from the Greek literally reads: *"Jesus is the Christ, the Son of the God."* That's our literal word-for-word translation from Greek. *Step Number 1.*

Step Number 2 is to make it sensible to the English reader, and put meaning to it we can understand. We also want it to be grammatically correct in our own language.

In this example, all we have to do is omit the word *"the,"* and it would read as we would understand it:

"Jesus is the Christ, the Son of God."

The close to John 20:31 should read:

Step 1- (literal translation):

"and, in order that believing, life you may be possessing in the name of him."

(Notice the word-order from Greek. In the next step, you must arrange the words and phrases to be grammatical and to make sense in English, without losing the meaning from Greek).

Step 2- (English meaning):

"and by reason of believing, you may possess life by means of his name."

Your translation is now complete. Congratulations. A job well done. Would you like to continue?

The next lesson dealing with translation will require a bit more concentration on your part, but don't worry, you will be guided every step of the way. Prepare yourself for a very enjoyable experience.

Our translating technique will scrutinize the diverse conjugations (inflections) of verbs. These changes will capture our attention as we see them in action.

Let us examine the Greek verb *"judge,"* κρίνω (**kree'**no, *"I judge"*) in its various declensions.

One good example is found at Matthew 7:1, 2:

Μὴ *κρίνετε,* ἵνα μὴ *κριθῆτε·* **2** ἐν ᾧ γὰρ *κρίματι* *κρίνετε* *κριθήσεσθε,* . . .

Here, there are **four forms** of the verb *κρίνω* and its related noun *κρίμα.* Let's translate:

Μὴ - "Not" (negative particle)

κρίνετε - "be you judging," (2nd person plural, present indicative or imperative active)

ἵνα - "with the intent that," or "for" (conjugation)

(Continued)

(Continued)

μὴ - "not", negative particle

κριθῆτε· - "you should be judged," 2nd person plural, aorist subjunctive passive

ἐν - "in," preposition

ᾧ - "what," dative singular masculine or neuter of ὃς

γὰρ - "for," conjunction

κρίματι - "judgment," dative singular noun

κρίνετε - "you are judging," 2nd person plural present indicative or imperative active

κριθήσεσθε - "you will be judged," 2nd person plural, future passive

It is fascinating to see the various forms of the word ***"judge,"*** and thus, be able to understand the important lesson Jesus is teaching us.

Let's put our literal word-for-word translation together to see what has been revealed to us:

*"Not be you **judging**, with the intent that not you should be **judged**; **2** in what for **judgment** you are **judging,** you will be **judged** . . ."*

Our first step of translating gives us some idea of what Jesus is saying, but we need to look more closely to get the clear meaning from the Greek.

Recall that μή is a particle of negation which is conditional. At Matthew 7:1, it is associated with the phrase *"be you judging."*

But the Greek goes farther than saying: **' Do not** *judge.'* The present imperative of the verb *"judge"* is not forbidding something not yet done; it is telling us to cease what *we have been doing*: *"**Stop** judging."*

With this in mind, let us put to work Step 2 and translate the Greek into its meaning in English:

*"**Stop** judging with the intent that you may not be judged, **2** for with what judgment you are judging, you yourself will be judged."*

Jesus' words make it clear that the individual who has rendered adverse personal judgments toward others, must ***cease*** being critical and faultfinding.

Translate verses 3-5, which illustrate the need to look at our brother in the proper light, and not self-righteously feel we have to remove the straw from his eye while ignoring the rafter in ours.

The *present imperative verb* certainly brings out the important lesson we must all learn on this matter.

(Notice its use at John 20:17. Jesus is not saying to Mary, *"Do **not** touch me,"* but *"**Stop** holding on to me,"* indicating she was clinging to his garment and was not letting go.)

You no doubt are finding our translating work very interesting, as well as informative.

Let's perform another exercise in translation. This time, we'll look at Luke's narrative of the apostle Paul's missionary work, as recorded at **Acts 20:1:**

Μετὰ δὲ τὸ παύσασθαι τὸν θόρυβον
μεταπεμψάμενος ὁ Παῦλος τοὺς
μαθητὰς καὶ παρακαλέσας
ἀσπασάμενος ἐξῆλθεν πορεύεσθαι
εἰς Μακεδονίαν.

Let's try a different format this time:

Μετὰ - **(After)** You will recognize our preposition friend who is always late.

δὲ τὸ - **(but the)** A conjunctive particle with the article denoting continuation in the narrative.

παύσασθαι - **(to cease)** A verb in the aorist infinitive tense, middle voice, noting a single act done to itself with durative results.

τὸν - The article "the" in the accusative
(the) case, which agrees with the noun.

θόρυβον - Noun, in the accusative, singular.
(commotion)

μεταπεμψάμενος - nominative singular
(having summoned masculine participle,
[to him]) aorist tense.

ὁ - The article "the," masculine,
(the) nominative singular.

Παῦλος - Proper name, nominative case.
(Paul)

τοὺς - The article "the," masculine,
(the) accusative plural.

μαθητὰς - Noun, accusative plural.
(disciples)

καὶ - Conjunction.
(and)

παρακαλέσας **(having encouraged)**	-	Nominative singular, masculine participle aorist.
ἀσπασάμενος **(having greeted)**	-	Nominative singular, masculine participle aorist.
ἐξῆλθεν **(he went out)**	-	Verb, 3rd person singular aorist indicative.
πορεύεσθαι **(to be going)**	-	Present infinitive
εἰς **(into)** 	-	Preposition, our "person" who did not mind her own business.
Μακεδονίαν **(Macedonia)**	-	Proper Noun, accusative case.

Do not be dismayed by the seemingly difficult words we have just considered. Greek is a beautiful language, and there is precious meaning hidden within the ocean bottom of God's Word. You will be delighted by the elegant finds of your studies.

As we have intended, we are continuing to make our course in Greek *enlightening* and *enjoyable*.

So, let's proceed with our translation of Acts 20:1, and see how our comprehension of the text comes smoothly:

Step 1: We must now compose our individual word translation into word-for-word phrases.

Using your notebook, see if you have copied each Greek word and placed it in the proper order that you translated from Greek.

It should read this way:

After but the to cease the commotion having summoned [to him] the Paul the disciples and having encouraged having greeted he went out to be going into Macedonia.

As your translating ability is increasing, you can certainly appreciate that there is more to translating than merely incorporating Step 1.

It is true, Step 1 has given you some semblance of meaning, but Step 2 makes the thought clear to the English reader.

Step 2: You may have a translation similar to the following:

Now after the commotion had ceased, Paul summoned the disciples, and when he had encouraged them, and given them his farewell, he went out to travel into Macedonia.

Don't worry if your translation is not exactly as the above, but it should contain elements which give accurate meaning to Paul's words.

How does it make you feel to have translated a few passages from the Scriptures? It provides a feeling of confidence and fulfillment, doesn't it.

(Note: It proves beneficial to write the Greek words in a notebook, because you will be able to become more familiar with the letters and words in this manner. They will thus be easier to identify.)

Before we conclude our chapter on translating, it would help your confidence level if we took a few moments to look at some of those apparently difficul words in our exercise at **Acts 20:1.**

Your knowledge of Greek will be enhanced as you *study* these words.

1- Three participles- Our verse contained three long words, which are **participles.** If you recall, participles are *verbal adjectives.*

An English equivalent may be "the Coming One." This expression *describes* and shows *action.* It encompasses the two functions.

The first *participle* at **Acts 20:1** is:

μεταπεμψάμενος
metapempsa'menos

We transliterated the word for you so that you can study it more carefully.

Let's break it down; it will greatly help us:

meta	**pempsa'**	**menos**
after	having summoned	(to him)

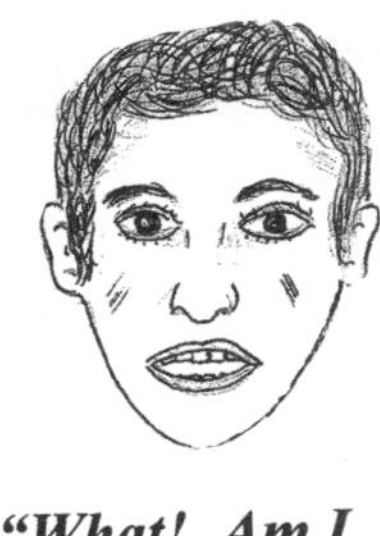

"What! Am I late again?"

You recognize our "late" preposition friend ***meta***, which means *"after."*

Pempsa is a form of the Greek word **pempto,** which is defined: *"to send (summon)."* (See your lexicon).

Menos is a suffix, which refers to the *person* who is the possessor of this description and action.

(Note: A clue to identifying many *participles* is observing this ending: *"**menos.**"*)

Now, that wasn't so hard, was it? If the word is broken down into syllables, it is easy to understand.

Let us look at the second *participle* at **Acts 20:1:**

παρακαλέσας

Once again, we provide you with our transliteration and a breakdown of the word:

para **ka·le'** **sas**
beside [he] encouraged (aorist ending)

Here is our gregarious preposition "friend" ***para,*** who likes to be *"with"*, or *"beside"* others.

*"I hope my being **with** you will be an **encouragement** to you."*

Ka·le' is a form of the verb ***ka·le'o***, and includes: *"to address, to speak words of encouragement."*

The aorist ending ***sas*** has no reference the time involved when the apostle Paul gave encouragement.

Is it becoming easier for you? Let's consider the third participle at **Acts 20:1:**

ἀσπασάμενος

a spa sa' men-os

The Greek *verb* ***a spa'zo-mai*** is the root word of our participle, and can either mean *"a greeting,"* or, as in this case, *"a farewell."*

Notice how this third *participle* ends with ***menos,*** which gives us a clue it is a *participle.*

Of course, participles can end with ***tos*** and ***teos.*** *(See Chapter 8 which discusses participles at length).*

2- Now, a little information regarding *two verbs* at **Acts 20:1:**

The verb ἐξῆλθεν **(ex-*eel'*-then),** *"he went out,"* is in the *aorist* tense. It denotes a single act by Paul, but does not specify *when*; yet, it is viewed as a whole event. *(See Chapter 6 on "Verbs.")*

It agrees with the *tense* of the *three participles* we just considered- *'the sending,' 'the encouraging,'* and the *'farewell greeting'* are in the *aorist* tense.

Finally, we would like to mention the *tense* of the Greek verb πορεύεσθαι **(po-rev' es·the),** *"to be going."* This verb is in the present *infinitive* tense

We briefly discussed the *infinitive* as a verbal noun in Chapter 6. It explains an interesting aspect of the verb, that of *unlimited duration.*

It is like the dative case in that it expresses *purpose*, and like the dative, frequently has the ending *αι.*

In Paul's case, *"he went out,"* leaving with purpose, but the infinitive allows his departure to be limitless

We will learn more about the fascinating *infinitve* in future studies.

As we close our chapter regarding translation, we hope it has inspired you to dive more readily into the pure waters of truth and discover many new things- *pearls* of high value for your lasting benefit.

But if you are to choose which *style* of translation, what would be your preference?

CHAPTER 11

YOUR *STYLE* OF TRANSLATION-WHICH DO YOU PREFER?

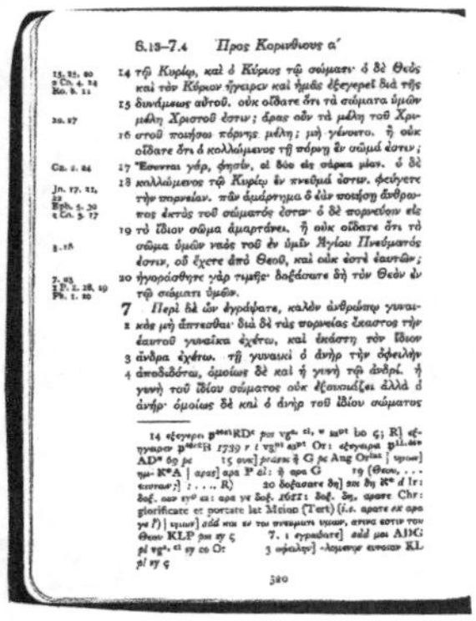

*N*ow that you possess the basics of Bible translation, which style do you prefer?

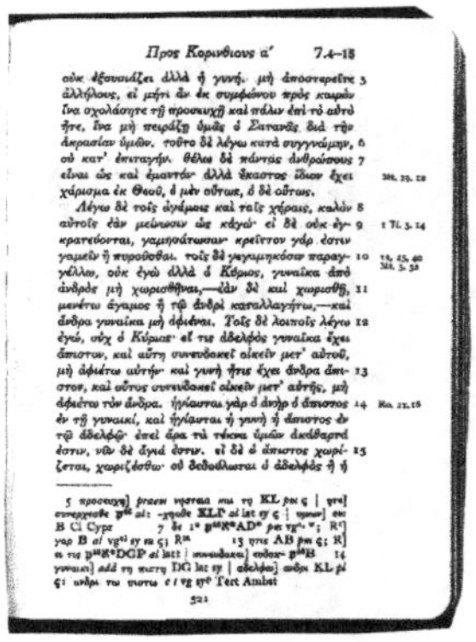

Will you use a style which adheres closely to the original translation, and which we used in our exercises? Or, will you opt for a free-spirited style, which embarks on a daring approach?

It is for these reasons, that there are numerous translations of the Bible available for the modern reader. We must realize that many translators have produced versions from their own perspective, and have, as a result of diligent research, chosen to include in their own translations, information which others have not viewed as important.

As long as their versions reveal hidden pearls within the Greek text, and remain true to the original, there should be no objection to their use. We need to keep an open mind in this regard.

Having a variety of Bible translations has its advantages. As Bible readers and translators, we can make comparisons and see how closely these versions capture the proper sense of the Greek.

There is a particular nuance, or shade of meaning, for some Greek words and phrases. Our examination of different translations will help us to see which ones have taken the time and effort to retrieve these "pearls." This research will broaden our knowledge.

1- Shades of Bible Greek

We can compare these variances to the shades of color in the color spectrum. In the red area, we have shades ranging from *light pink* to *dark crimson* (with many reds in between). Within the blue portion, we find *pastel* all the way to *indigo* and *Navy blue.*

In a similar fashion, Greek words describe variances, conveying a particular meaning according to a number of factors: (1) Context; (2) History; and (3) its general use in the Scriptures.

For instance, the Greek word translated *"world"* is ***kosmos*** (κόσμος), from which we derive our words "*cosmetics*," makeup, and "*cosmos*," universe, giving us the sense of *order*. Writers of Bible Greek used the word to describe "people, mankind" in an orderly arrangement, sometimes in opposition to God.

A Greek word that is similar, but with a varied shade of meaning is ***aion*** (αἰών). Scholars translate this word as "age, era, epoch." It defines any period in human history with its unique characteristics.

A related Greek word is ***oikoumene*** (οἰκουμένη), and is translated "inhabited earth." It gives reference to earth as inhabited by mankind.

The literal globe itself, and its land translate the Greek word ***ge*** (γῆ). From this, we acquire our word ***ge***ography, our study of the earth.

All four words have one thing in common: People and their place of dwelling. But all allude to different aspects of *mankind* and his *home.*

 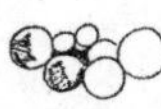 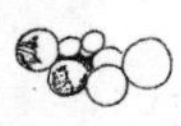 

Other examples of Greek nuances include use of *four* Greek words for ***love***.
Agape (ἀγάπη) means love based on *principle*; concern for the welfare of others. Jesus used this kind of love more often than any other. (John 3:16; 21:15, 16; Matthew 5:44; 22:37, 38)

There is also the love of *warm affection*, a tender attachment to another. This is the Greek word ***philia*** (φιλία) and entails cherishing another. It is used in the third of Jesus' three questions to Peter: *"Do you have affection for me?"* (John 21:17)

Another shade of love refers to love for *family*, expressed in the Greek word ***storge*** (στοργή). In the Greek text, this word is in its negative form ***astorge*** at Romans 1:31 and at 2 Timothy 3:3, where it can be translated *"no familial affection."* It is also seen in compound form with *philia* at Romans 12:10.

A fourth kind of love is ***eros***, a romantic love for someone with whom one contemplates marriage. "*New Testament*" writers did not see a reason for using ***eros***. However, the Greek *Septuagint* (an early Greek translation of the "*Old Testament*") includes forms of the word at Proverbs 7:18 and 30:16.

It should be noted that married couples should work hard at cultivating all four kinds of *love,* with special emphasis on the kind of love God and Christ have shown us, ***agape*** love. (Eph. 5:25; 1 John 4:10).

The foregoing examples, illustrating the different shades of meaning, should assist us in seeing, not merely the beauty of the Greek language, but the profounds truths of God's Word which mold our lives in a beneficial way.

Our knowledge of these *"pearls"* that were previously protected within the deep recesses of the sacred text of Bible Greek, is truly enhanced. As a consequence, our interest and love for the Author and His Sacred Scriptures is deepened.

2- *Constant Need for New and Revised Translations*

If you are a person who possesses traditional versions like *the King James Version* or the Catholic *Douay Version,* you may believe that no other Bible translation can surpass these older versions.

There can be no question that these translations have served Bible lovers well over the centuries, helping millions to come to understand the Word of God. Their poetic expressions and traditional renderings, as those in the Lord's Prayer, or, the Our Father Prayer, are cherished and repeated by vast numbers of humanity, as is the beloved twenty-third Psalm.

It may seem strange to some that a need exists for new Bible translations, but this is the case today.

Psalm 23

The Lord is my shepherd;
I shall not want.
2 He maketh me to lie down
in green pastures;
He leadeth me beside the
still waters.
3 He restoreth my soul;
He leadeth me in the paths of
righteousness for his
name's sake.

One can remain faithful to his traditional version and, yet, be open to new versions.

How can this be so? Bible scholars and translators recognize there are at least *three* good reasons for up-to-date translations:

(1) Since the 19th Century, archaeologists have discovered older and more accurate Bible manuscripts, and these have been made available to Bible scholars.

(2) With a greater number of Greek manuscripts of the "*New Testament,*" in addition to non-Biblical writings of *Koine* Greek, at our disposal, our knowledge of Bible languages is greatly increased.

(3) The language of older translations, especially those of centuries past, becomes harder to understand as that language changes in the course of time.

These are important reasons for considering the value of modern translations, while, at the same time, remaining faithful to our older versions.

When the *King James Version* was produced in 1611 there were only a few Greek manuscripts available, and these were of rather late origin.

All the writings of the Greek "*New Testament*" were written in the First Century. Manuscript copie which are closer in time to the originals are more accurate, for there would be less time for errors to creep into the Greek text.

ΗΑΓΝΟΕΙΤΕΑΔ
ΟΝΟΜΟΣΚΥΠΙ
ΖΗΗΓΑΠΥΠΑΝ
ΝΟΜΩΕΑΝΔΕΑ
ΟΑΝΗΡΚΑΤΗΠ
ΑΡΑΟΥΝΖΩΝΤ
ΞΠΗΜΑΤΙΣΕΙΕ
ΕΛΕΥΘΕΠΑΕΣ
ΜΟΙΞΑΛΙΔΑΓΙ
ΑΔΕΛΠΗΟΙΜΟ
ΣΟΜΑΤΟΣΤΟΥ

With what has been uncovered in recent years, we have the privilege of examining copies which are older, and thus, less affected by scribal errors. We can feel confident we now possess more reliable copies of the Bible.

There are presently over 5,000 Greek manuscript copies of the "*New Testament*" in the possession of Bible scholars and institutions. The known oldest is a fragment of a copy of the Gospel of John, which dates to the Second Century. Parts of the Book of Matthew may possibly be from the First Century!

3- Which Style of Translation Will You Choose?

Because you are interested in learning Bible Greek, you are the sort of person who is open to *new* things.

Among those *new* things is your desire to translate from the original Greek. Becoming acquainted with grammar, you can make a comparison between your new-found knowledge and existing Bible translations, such as your own.

Your purpose in doing so is not to be critical of these versions, but to check for accuracy. This will increase your Bible knowledge.

So, as a translator, you have *two main choices* in your *style* of translation:

(1) literal, or (2) Paraphrase.

The **literal** translation has as its objective to adhere as closely as possible to the original language form.

The **paraphrase** style endeavors to convey the message from the original text, in its own words, using all available resources, often to give clarity to the meaning from the translator's perspective.

Put another way: A **literal** translation centers on the Greek text itself, while the **paraphrase** translation directs itself to the mind of the reader.

In either case, the translator must determine that the true sense of the text is not lost, but expressed clearly, as the original writer had intended.

Literal translations cannot be too literal, because, as we have seen during our translation exercises, Greek is different from English.

However, if a **literal** style is chosen, consistency in the use of Greek words, should be rendered by the same English word, according to its context.

If you choose the **paraphrase** style, you will have greater freedom, but try to stick to the basic text.

There are some dangers in the **paraphrase** style. Each Bible writer had his own particular style, even changing his style, in some places.

It is difficult to translate accurately using an **paraphrase** style if the Bible writer composed his writings and had his own word choice different from that of other writers.

Another danger of the **paraphrase** style lies in giving a free or loose rendering of the text to the extent it is totally foreign to the original.

Let's use the example of *John 3:16*. If we choose the **paraphrase** style, we need to exercise caution so that our translation does not read something like this:

"Now, God was sentimental enough with us that he handed over his Son living in cushy comfort, so anybody who appreciates what he did won't be classed as an ingrate, but be in his good graces."

This, of course, is an exaggeration, but it demonstrates what can occur when a translator takes too many liberties in this translation style.

"If Son you are of the God, say in order that stones these loaves may become." ⇦ On, the other hand, embracing too closely the **literal** style would create a stilted, inflexible version, hard to read.

So perhaps a style you may prefer would be one which incorporates *both styles*, containing elements of the **literal** and those of the **paraphrase.**

But if you decide on either of the two styles, please remember: *Make it interesting, make it flowing, and most important of all, make it* ***accurate.***

Yes, new Bible translations are needed, for the knowledge of God and His Son continues to increase. Jesus stated at John 17:3: *"This is what everlasting life means, their* (Jesus' followers) ***continually taking in knowledge*** (Greek- γινώσκωσι, present tense) *of you, the only true God, and Jesus Christ, whom you sent forth."*

CHAPTER 12

DISCOVERING UNIQUE "PEARLS IN DEEP, CLEAR WATERS"

Our course in Greek has been most enlightening. We have acquired an elementary understanding of this unique language in which a portion of the Holy Scriptures was inspired to be written.

For the student of Greek, *Koine* is a living tongue with a living message. Our investigation has taken us to the clear depths of God's Word, and we have found a number of valuable "pearls."

This is similar to what is being found currently in South Sea oysters- beautiful black pearls, measuring from 14 to 20 millimeters in size. These unique gems are truly a prized possession, as are mother-of-pearls, with their many variations in hue.

In this chapter, we will touch on a few *exclusive* pearls, those hard to find. But when we locate these, we will be enthralled by *unique* discoveries.

One of these is found in the literal meaning of the Greek word translated "forgive" at Matthew 6:14. Here, the word in Greek is ἀφῆτε and literally means *"you might send off [from yourself]."*

Our lexicon tells us this word is *2 person plural aorist 2, subjunctive mood, active voice.* This information reveals a wealth of knowledge. Let us analyze it and we will see a deep truth revealed to us.

Jesus addresses his words to "you," *second person plural;* that is, to his disciples and others present when he was giving his famous Sermon on the Mount. He had just instructed them how the pray, using the Lord's Prayer as a model, including the request to God for the forgiveness of their sins.

Now in verses 14 and 15, he shows them the conditions God gives for His forgiving sins:

"For if you forgive [ἀφῆτε] men their trespasses, your heavenly Father will also forgive you; but if you do not forgive [ἀφῆτε] men their trespasses, neither will your Father forgive your trespasses."

Jesus shows how vital it is for us to show true forgiveness to others when they sin against us. The *aorist* tense suggests a single act performed, without reference to time. Jesus is making it plain we must perform the gracious act of forgiveness promptly and completely if we are to expect our Father's forgiveness for our many sins.

The *subjunctive mood* of ἀφῆτε tells us that this is a possibility on our part, leaving the decision up to us. That is why the literal meaning of this Greek word is: *"you **might** send off [from yourself]."* And it is in the *active voice,* revealing that we, the ones, addressed, would be wise to do something.

But why is ἀφῆτε translated by the phrase *"you might **send off**"?* What does this mean? It means *letting go* of an offense, making it leave our hearts, and not allowing resentment any longer to exist within us. And we overlook others' shortcomings.

A form of this Greek word is used at Matthew 8:15, where Jesus healed Peter's mother-in-law. The Greek phrase rendered in English is *"left her the fever."* The fever went out from her and was no longer within her.

And, so, with the offenses and sins others commit against us, we forgive them, or *'send them off,'* and making them ineffective, such as a fever leaving us.

Scholars recognize this is a fundamental meaning of *"ἀφίημι" ("to let leave from")* in the Scriptures. This means *"to send away [as from oneself]."* Thus, we **separate in our minds** the sin from the one who sinned against us. When we see that person, we do not see the sin. We have dismissed it from our minds

We do not wish to be the kind of person Jesus describes at Luke 7:48: *"He who is forgiven little, loves little."* If one is *"forgiven little" (passive voice)* by God, it means the person is under the mistaken notion, he sins little, and hardly needs forgiveness. So, his self-righteousness leads him to love little.

This "pearl" of truth is valuable for us if we are to maintain a close relationship with God and others.

Shall we look closely at other *exclusive* pearls? They have to do with the *writing style* and *word choice* of the Gospel writers.

Matthew, Mark, and Luke relate the account of a woman whose persistent hemorrhaging Jesus healed. (Matt. 9:19-22; Mark 5:25-34; Luke 8:43-48).

While the Christ was on his way to heal the dying daughter of Jairus, the woman, suffering from her twelve-year ailment, approached God's Son from behind and touched the fringe of his outer garment. *"Instantly,"* the account at Luke 8:44 tells us, *"her flow of blood stopped."*

Jesus, sensing power went out from him, said: *"Someone touched me."* The woman came trembling before him and falling at his feet, confessed before all what she had done. Jesus, noting her sincerity and honesty, told her that her faith had made her well.

Matthew's description of Jesus' act of healing makes use of the Greek word σώζω ("to save").

Properly translated in this context, σώζω means: *"to get well."* The thought being that the one who is healed is *saved* from disease and its effects. Of note, is the fact that three forms of this Greek word are used in this account.

Apparently, Matthew, who is writing to Jews to prove that Jesus is the promised Messiah, centers on the saving power of Jesus, both physically and spiritually. For instance, it is Matthew who records God's angel appearing to Joseph in a dream and saying Mary would *"give birth to a son, and you must call his name Jesus, for he will* ***save*** *his people from their sins."* (Matthew 1:21)

In Mark's narrative of this account (which is the most descriptive of the three), he, too, uses the Greek word translated *"save."* But Mark also incorporates a common Greek word to denote healing: ἴαται, a verb in the 3rd person singular perfect indicative passive, which means *"she has been healed."* (Mark 5:29). It's root is ἰάομαι, and often relates to physical healing. In verse 26, Mark calls the physicians whom the woman consulted as ἰατρῶν. ("healers"). Mark was writing to Romans who would appreciate the value of a true healer, since so many pseudo-healers were prevalent in the Roman world, and his readers could well relate to the fact that the woman described in his account had been so unsuccessful in finding a cure for her illness. Her experience would impress honest-hearted Romans, and help them appreciate that this Jesus was a genuine healer. It would give them reason to investigate to see if he was really the Christ.

The writer Luke, who is also called ὁ ἰατρὸς (*"the physician"*), at Colossians 4:14, includes the moving experience of the ailing woman in his narrative. But, as a physician, writing to a noted "Theophilus," he would utilize *three* words to describe Jesus' healing of this woman. (Luke 8:43-48)

He relates: *"she was healed,"* (Gr- ἰάθη, 3rd person singular *aorist* indicative passive). Luke notes the woman confessed her *action*, which resulted in her healing, and Jesus' kind response: *"Daughter, your faith* ***has made you well*** (Gr- σέσωκέν σε, 3rd person singular perfect indicative active), or, *"has* *saved you."* Her faith had *completed* her *action*. She was now healed, *saved* from her twelve-year sickness, and was free to go on her way.

But earlier, in verse 43, Luke uses a *third* Greek word which describes healing. There, we read that the woman *"had not been able to get a* **cure** *from anyone."* The Greek **verb** translated *"cure"* is θεραπεύω, and is used in English today in the words "therapy." and "therapeudic."

This Greek word is associated with one who serves as an *attendant*, or who cares for, and treats the sick. It is used more frequently in the Gospels than other Greek words in cases where Jesus touched and personally treated the ill and those with infirmities. (Matt. 8:7; 15:30; 17:16; 19:2; 21:14; Mark 3:2,10; 6:5; Luke 4:40; 5:15; 13:14; John 5:10).

While the apostle John did not refer to this particular woman in his account, he, nevertheless, recounts Jesus' acts of healing. It is interesting that John uses a *fourth* word to explain what Jesus did. It is the Greek word ὑγιής, and means: "sound in health."

This word has specific reference to making a person whole, emphasizing the process by which the individual is completely healed.

The case mentioned at John Chapter 5 applies in that manner. A man, sick for thirty-eight years, had not been able to walk. Jesus made him sound in health, or, whole, and the man was able to walk again.

Matthew uses ὑγιής just once (12:13*), in the case of God's Son healing a man with a withered hand, telling us his hand *"was restored **sound** like the other hand."* He was completely healed.

It must be stated, in passing, that the four Gospel writers made use of all these words in their accounts of Jesus' miraculous healings. But in certain instances, they concentrated on selective words to characterize the form of healing Jesus employed.

These pearls of truth, with their many hues, paint a beautiful picture of a loving, compassionate, and self-sacrificing Messiah who delighted in making

* One outstandingly accurate Greek text contains this Greek word only one time in the book of Matthew.

persons well and sound again. In all cases, those healed had never felt better in their lives. No doubt this made them quite interested when God's Son spoke to them about *everlasting life*.

The Gospel writers, with their unique styles, and under the influence of God's holy spirit, illuminated the true nature of Jesus' teachings, using the special features of *Koine* Greek, which provide us with pearls of outstanding value.

Incidentally, the Greek words ἰατρὸς (physician), and θεραπεύω (therapy) are also used in Modern Greek.

As we further explore the depths of these clear waters, we come upon another significant pearl. We find it in the coves of several Bible passages. It is the Greek word καλός. If we translate this word as "good," we would not be seeing this pearl in its proper hue. καλός has a deeper meaning. It is true, it is "good," but to a superlative degree.

Scholars observe καλός as something intrinsically good, and which, within its circumstances, is well adapted. It is described as beautiful, excellent, choice, select. So, instead of Jesus speaking of *"good fruit"* at Matthew 7:17, 19, he is really referring to it as *"choice, select, fine"* fruit.

When he speaks about *"a good tree"* producing "choice fruit," the tree can be accurately described as "good." Here, the correct Greek word for "good," ἀγαθόν (accusative case) is used, which scholars define as good in nature and constitution.

But the fruit (καρπούς), picturing Christian works of faith, is *excellent* by nature. It is *wholesome*, it is *approved* by God. Therefore, the fruit is *choice, select, fine*.

The Greek adjectives καλός and ἀγαθός mean basically the same thing, but the former is, in essence, expressing that quality to a greater degree than the latter.

Consequently, the description Jesus applies to himself at John 10:11 would be of greater worth than "good." As ὁ ποιμὴν ὁ καλός, he is our shepherd with *excellent* credentials. He is, as the Greek adjective καλός so well describes: "the *elegant*, *exquisite*, *handsome, pleasing* shepherd." You can also use excelling adjectives as *genuine, noble, admirable, fine, honorable.* These reveal the full import of this unique Greek word.

Sometimes pearls may seem to have the same color, or hue, but when scrutinized more closely, reveal a shade not seen before.

This is also true of many Greek words. We have considered some of these variances, but a very interesting one concerns the use of nouns relating to *young children.* Studying these will enlighten us regarding many vital Bible subjects.

Let's start with the Greek word βρέφος. It can mean either the *unborn* (Luke 1:41), or a *newborn* child. (Luke 2:12, 16). When Timothy's mother and grandmother taught him Christian values, he learned them *"from infancy (Gr- βρέφους)."* (2 Tim. 3:15). So, from a very early age, Timothy was taught the sacred writings, which played a key role in his development as an outstanding Christian man.

This is an area where modern parents can take note. Scientists recognize that neural connections in an infant's brain are formed very early, receptive to vital information which shapes the child's thought patterns.

Another Greek word, παιδίον, has reference to a *"young child,"* ranging from infancy to mature childhood. This word is found at Matthew 2: 8, 11,13, 14, 16, 20 where we read the account about the magi (or, astrologers) visiting the child Jesus.

Observe in verse 16, where King Herod sought to destroy young boys two years of age and under. Matthew's use of the Greek παιδίον in this setting reveals Jesus was past being a newborn when the magi arrived, and was approximately the age of two. This would mean their visit was about two years later than the date popularly held .

Unquestionably, the Greek shows a shade of the pearl we may have not seen before, and helps us to explain accurately the events in Jesus' earthly life.

Νήπιος is a Greek word which also can mean little child, *"a babe"* (Matt. 21:16; 1 Cor. 13:11).

But this word is generally used in a metaphorical sense, indicating one who is *unskilled,* or *untaught.* Christians are to grow spiritually, and not be deceived by false teachings (1 Cor. 3:1; Eph. 4:14).

In addition, νηπίοις *(plural)* can have reference to full-grown Christians who are not viewed as mature by worldly intellectuals. (Matt. 11:25).

Still other words identifying children are:

τέκνον - an offspring, one who is a descendant, one's posterity. (Matt. 2:18; 3:9; 10:21); figuratively (John 1:12; Eph. 5:8). This word stresses the *birth* of the individual.

τεκνίον - *"Little child."* Used only figuratively in the Greek text, where a teacher may address his students or disciples. (John13:33; Galatians 4:19)

υἱός - A son. This word emphasizes the dignity and nature of the relationship. But also in a literal sense, it means one who is the male issue from his parents. (Matt. 10:37; John 3:16; Acts 7:29).

ἄρσεν - A male. (Luke 2:23; Rev. 12:5, 13).

Everyone of these Greek words describing children assist us to draw on the relationships we need to maintain with our loved ones, and that which we must have with our heavenly Father and His Son.

We shall conclude this search for unique pearls within these waters with the consideration of a text which leaves absent the definite article.

A well-known verse, if not translated properly, would overlook important Bible truths. It is found at 1 Timothy 6:10. According to the Greek, it reads:

ῥίζα	γὰρ	πάντων	τῶν	κακῶν
a root	for	of all	the	malicious (things)

ἐστὶν	ἡ	φιλαργυρία,
is	the	cherishing of silver,

With all due respect for traditional translations, they do not convey the true meaning of Paul's words. Some have Paul saying: "***Money*** *is the root of all evil.*" But the Greek noun, which is a compound word, means an affection *(philia)* of money *(silver).*

The Bible does not condemn the use and possession of money, even as Jesus himself indicated a number of times. (Matt. 17:27; 22:19; Luke 15:9).

It is the insatiable *thirst* and *lust* for money which Jesus and his disciples condemn, a *cherishing* of it, which neglects any possible affection for God and neighbor. (See Luke 12:16-21; 16:14; 2 Tim. 3:2).

But the point we wish to stress even more in this scripture is the *absence* of the article before the noun ῥίζα (root). What is the point?

This: the love of money is *only one root* ("***a*** root") of many things which can cause us great spiritual harm and ruin. We must combat these malicious traits.

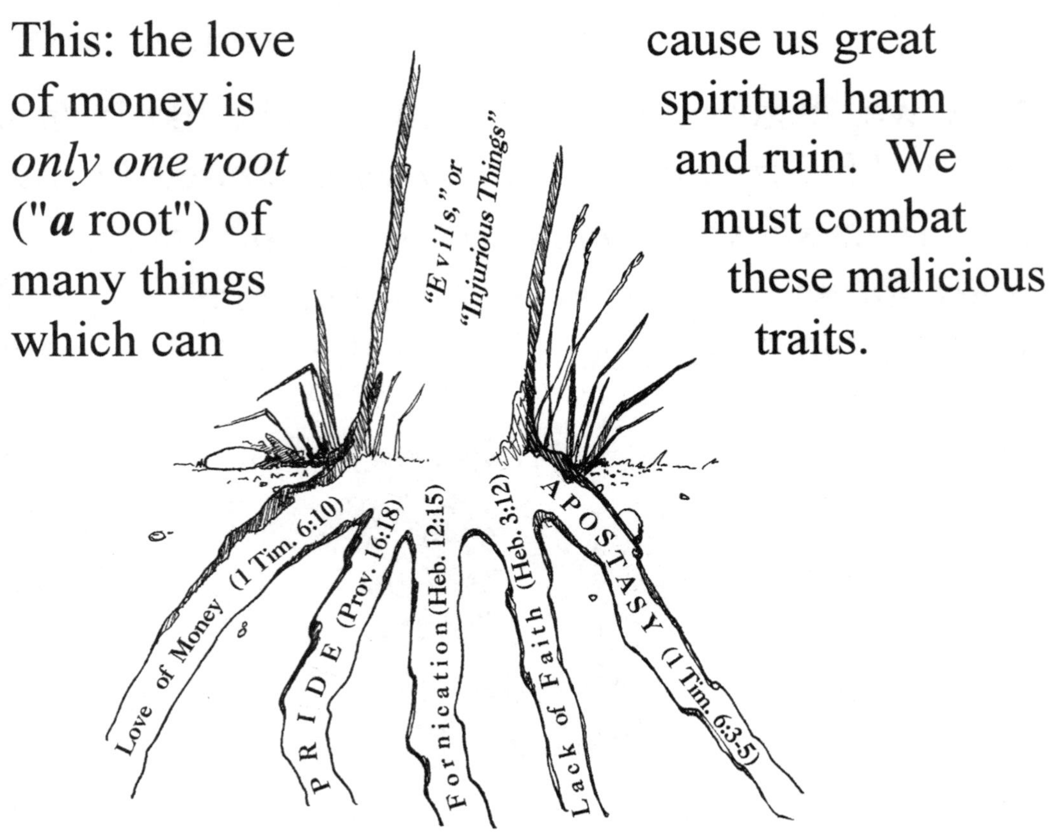

True, the love of money is certainly a deadly root, as Paul disclosed in the remainder of verse 10. But other things, such as fornication (illicit sex), pride, lack of faith, apostasy from the Christian faith, as well as additional sins, are *roots* which grow in the heart and which bring us severe spiritual injury. (Heb. 3:12; 12:15; Prov. 16:18; 1 Timothy 6:3-5). If not corrected, such poisonous roots can snuff out any desire we may have for studying theWord of God. May that never happen to us!

May we, instead, prove ourselves to be like a *"tree planted by streams of water, that produces its own fruit in its season, which comprises foliage that does not wither, and everything that one does will without fail be successful."* (Psalm 1:3)

CONCLUSION

This, dear friend, is our introductory course to ***Koine*** Greek. The author hopes you have found it comparatively *easy* as well as *fun.* True, a subject of this nature requires much thought and careful examination. It is recommended that you repeat this course to gain the utmost benefit. This would especially be necessary if you are having some difficulty understanding it.

But if you took the time to follow the suggestions contained in this primer, and utilized the resources made available to you, there can be no question you have learned the *basics* of Bible Greek.

Yes, it has required some investment- your precious time and resources. But have you not found your project worthwhile? Have you not delighted in your discovery of those figurative *"pearls"* (Greek- μαργαρῖται), some unique, lodged for so long in the deeper recesses of the ***Koine*** Greek of the Sacred Scriptures?

Now that you've acquired your diver's "lungs," you You can continue your dives with increased frequency and to greater depths.

Your confidence level should be fairly high by now, but even though you have reached the end of this publication, it is not the time to slow down or quit. Remember, this has been your quest for quite a long time, so don't view it as a lesser important pursuit now. Use your knowledge as a springboard to gain more knowledge- *full* or *accurate* knowledge.

But, please, don't use it to puff yourself up. Don't feel you are now superior to others. Rather, show a self-sacrificing spirit, and assist them to appreciate what a precious possession they may acquire.

May you have God's blessing, as you go on:

αὐξανόμενοι	τῇ	ἐπιγνώσει
growing	***to the***	***thorough knowledge***

τοῦ	θεοῦ·	
of the	***God.*** -	*Colossians 1:10.*

A

B

C

D

E

F

G

H

I

J

K

L

M

N

O

(Continued next column)

P

PARTS of the HUMAN ANATOMY

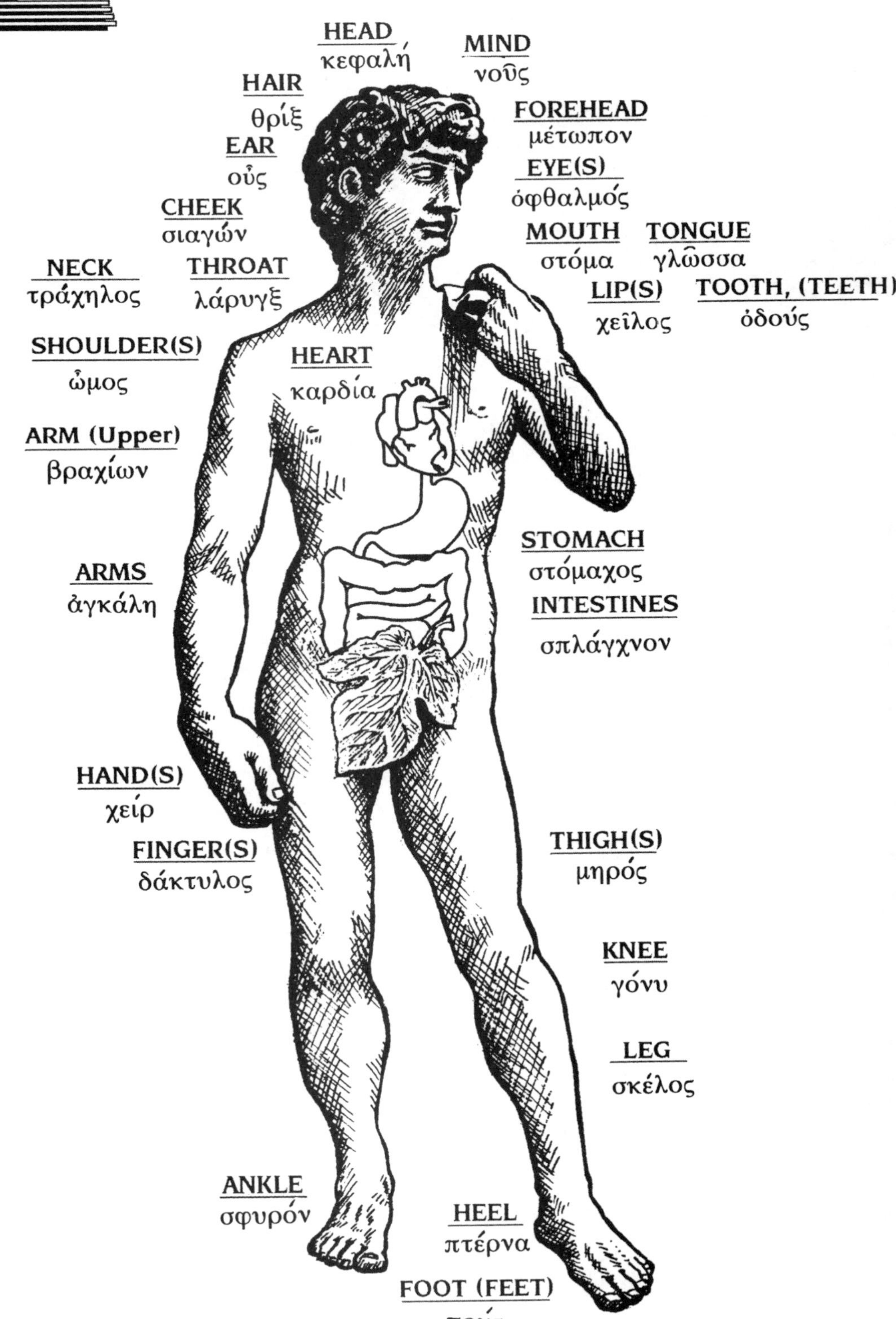

ABOUT THE AUTHOR

John Poly has been a minister and Bible educator for over 50 years, as well as an experienced public speaker. He has developed a deep interest in the languages of the Bible and modern Greek as the result of his years of research into numerous Bible translations, reference works, lexicons, grammars, and Greek interlinear translations.

The author's parents were Greek immigrants from the Mediterranean island of Cyprus. He and his brother and two sisters were born in New York City, and have lived in different parts of the country, including Norfolk, Virginia, where another sister was born. However, John has never visited the birthplace of his parents. It is a dream he hopes will come true some day.

Comparing the Greek of the Bible, especially the *"New Testament,"* with his knowledge of modern Greek, the author has personally seen a remarkable likeness. He has been able to identify with many words his parents spoke in regular conversations with the family, and which John has discovered with amazement in various Greek interlinear translations of the *"New Testament."* Though there is a difference in spelling and sentence structure in some of the words of the two Greek languages, there is a striking similarity and a direct link between them, and this is what John vividly shows in his introduction to Bible Greek. Most important of all, by means of a clear, understandable method, John assists inquisitive readers to acquire the ability to learn and read the *Koine* Greek of the *"New Testament."*

NOTES

NOTES

NOTES

NOTES

NOTES

NOTES